The Revd Andrew Procter                    rch of England minister,
has served as a member                      for health and healing,
and as the bishop's                          A professionally quali-
fied counsellor                              accredited membership of
the British A                                , and Psychotherapy, he serves
as a part-ti                                 Christian counselling service. He
is the author                                , the Vines (Redemptorist Press, 2005)
and co-author,                        eth, of Encountering Depression (SPCK,
2012), The Essentia.         ae to Burnout (Lion, 2013) and Exploring God
(Kevin Mayhew Publishers, 2003).

Dr Elizabeth Procter specialized in child and adolescent psychiatry
and has been a consultant psychiatrist for over fifteen years. Together
with Andrew, she has a vast experience of parish life, has led prayer
counselling teams and was a member of her diocesan council for health
and healing. She is a pastoral adviser to the bishop, helping to interview prospective ordinands, and has been a trustee of Burrswood
Christian Hospital. She has had several articles published in medical
journals and Christian magazines.

They have four adult children and five grandchildren.

# PRACTICAL HELP FOR STRESSED CHRISTIANS

*Your questions answered*

Andrew and Elizabeth Procter

First published in Great Britain in 2015

Society for Promoting Christian Knowledge
36 Causton Street
London SW1P 4ST
www.spck.org.uk

*British Library Cataloguing-in-Publication Data*
A catalogue record for this book is available from the British Library

ISBN 978–0–281–07242–2
eBook ISBN 978–0–281–07243–9

Typeset by Graphicraft Limited, Hong Kong
First printed in Great Britain by Ashford Colour Press
Subsequently digitally printed in Great Britain

eBook by Graphicraft Limited, Hong Kong

Produced on paper from sustainable forests

*To our grandchildren*

# Contents

——•◆•——

# Contents

## Part 5
## WORK

## Part 6

## CULTURE AND SOCIETY

# *Acknowledgements*

———◆·◆·◆———

Our thanks to Helen Leach and Kate Mendez for their help and input, and to all of those who willingly shared their stories with us.

# *Introduction*

As a Christian minister (Andrew) and doctor (Elizabeth), husband and wife team, we recently wrote a volume on burnout and overstress for a strictly secular readership. It became clear to us in the process that there are many factors in modern society that are big sources of additional stress for Christians. We felt it would be good to help people acknowledge these, and to draw on the riches of the Christian tradition in showing how stresses and strains may in fact contribute to our growth in faith, hope and love. We trust that if you are finding your life and your faith are getting just too much at the moment, this book will provide reassurance and inspiration.

Please don't think we reckon to have all the answers. We had to guard as best we could against getting stressed out ourselves writing the book, deluged as we suddenly seemed to be with family and professional matters coming from nowhere. But that is the reality of life, as you can no doubt appreciate! We feel we got through with a good deal of God's help and so, we are sure, will you.

There are many true stories in the book, and we're grateful to those who have given permission for their inclusion. Names have been changed throughout to preserve anonymity.

## *Stress factors*

Stress is now a huge factor in modern living. A recent survey estimates one-third of British workers will suffer from it at some stage in their careers.[1] There are great numbers of people on antidepressants (two million prescriptions for them were issued by the NHS in 2011), while 6.5 million working days a year are lost with employees off sick with stress. As Christians we are not immune: we too may be endeavouring to balance high-pressure working lives with looking after a family, earning our way in difficult times and so on. And we are vulnerable to additional factors that may increase our stress burden if not wisely addressed. A rough list, using the motif of 'expectations', would go as follows.

## God expectations

If we understand life in terms of loving and serving God, any general stress we are suffering from is likely to be compounded by a fear of failing God. It is all too easy to push ourselves beyond what is reasonable out of a sense of duty, which may result in guilt at taking perfectly reasonable downtime. It might get to the stage where we feel our faith is failing and that we are in danger of losing our salvation. This will add considerably to the existing difficulty of overstress.

## Church expectations

Christians are encouraged to go to church. Our local church, however, may be struggling to survive. There is likely to be a critical shortage of willing helpers and of enough money to keep the place going, and we may feel obliged to offer a serious sacrifice of time, resources and energy so as not to let down our minster or fellow church members. Service in the church can be a wonderfully enriching experience, but when our stress levels are already at a dangerous level, others' expectations can add considerably to the pressure we're under. This is to say nothing of the impact of church politics which, despite a veneer of 'defending the faith', can be bitter and vicious. All in all we may begin to find it difficult to attend church regularly, and then feel guilty for not doing so, increasing our stress levels even further.

## Societal expectations

It is no longer normal to be an active Christian in general society. Those of us who live out our faith openly will be seen as different to say the least. 'You don't go to church do you?' was asked with incredulity and some disdain of an ordinary part-time working mother at our church, when she explained to her work colleagues that she was going to be confirmed. It took some courage for her to stick to her guns, and she's now regarded as 'different' from those she works alongside. Her experience is similar to that of many as they move around in ordinary society. Christianity has always attracted some suspicion, but latterly we have seen more overt hostility to the Church in media coverage of national church affairs, court cases involving Christians whose faith has got them into trouble and the like. It all adds to the pressure.

## Workplace expectations

Research on overstress shows that idealistic, compassionate people are particularly vulnerable to burnout, and that those who choose to work in the caring professions tend to suffer more than those in commerce. This is probably because working with people is more stress inducing than working with commercial products. There is not an obvious end product in the former case, and people can be stubbornly difficult to help. The leading, identifiable high-risk group for overstress is idealistic members of the caring professions who work very hard, often badly under-resourced, for tens of years and then become vulnerable to emotional exhaustion and breakdown. Christians are more highly represented in health, teaching, social work and community building than in the commercial world. Their idealism and wish to do good very commendably takes them into these fields. So in this sense Christians are more vulnerable to overstress than others.

## Cultural expectations

Our society is now pluralistic. The old certainties are gone. A nation that was broadly Christian has all but disappeared. The background wallpaper of society has ceased to be instinctively favourable to our faith. Arguably it is ever more hostile. There is an aggressive atheism that is gaining support. The other world faiths are much more on the scene in national life than ever before. All this can be puzzling and dispiriting for Christians. They can wonder just what to believe any more. If they do hold to their certainties then they can be regarded as intolerant of others' views and out of touch. An example of this would be the area of sexuality. The Christian ideal of sex only within marriage is just a joke culturally. Marriage itself is waning as a cultural norm. The Church is wrestling with what to make of homosexuality and regarded as culturally out of touch by not agreeing to homosexual marriage. For a Christian already under considerable stress in their personal, professional and local church life, this cultural alienation can add to their sense of despair.

Given these factors it is not surprising that stress levels among Christians are high. Bishops too, and other denominational leaders, are ever more concerned that clergy stress is soaring. There is considerable incidence of stress-related sickness and emotional breakdown among them and their spouses. A recent survey on clergy stress commissioned by St Luke's Healthcare for Clergy reported that one-third of those surveyed were feeling seriously stressed and requested help.[2] Not researched as it ought to be is the stress incidence among highly motivated lay Christians. We suspect it too would be considerable.

## *The structure of the book*

This book is divided into six parts: Part 1 is about stress in general; Part 2 about stress to do with our relationship with God; Part 3 about stresses in family life; Part 4 about stress in church life; Part 5 about stress in the workplace; Part 6 about the stress of living in our increasingly anti-Christian culture.

Each of the 14 chapters answers a commonly asked question and is divided into four sections. The first section gives basic information about the problem raised in the chapter's title. The second looks at opportunities to address stress levels, with a mix of measuring exercises to plot your level of need and suggested activities and helpful ways to de-stress. The third section offers something by way of encouragement or inspiration, most likely a story of a Christian whose experience is especially germane to the chapter but perhaps something humorous or drawn from Christian tradition or public life. The fourth section provides some biblical material for meditation/reflection on the problem.

At the end of each chapter is a 'Stressbuster'. These are very short, simple, practical suggestions that we hope will be helpful in lowering stress levels. Sometimes they connect with the theme of the chapter, sometimes not.

The book can be read in any order and there is a section at the end giving available resources pertinent to each of the six parts of the book – these allow you to take things further if you wish.

## A few final thoughts . . .

We suggest that as you go through the book you may find it helpful to do three things:

### *Find a nice place and time in which to read it*

This might be somewhere in your home, as you commute, your local library or a favourite coffee shop – wherever, so long as it's a congenial place for you to relax and feel unhurried as you read. If your nice place is private enough, it may be that the meditations given in the book can be done there too, and so your nice place becomes a place of prayerfulness and sanctuary. And do give yourself time to take it in. Many of the stress factors we look at in the book are linked to lack of time. Don't try to take in this book as an extra, crammed in somewhere in the corners of your schedule, but decide to carve out delineated time in a pleasant environment in which to read it. You may find this contributes as much to easing your stress as does the content of the book. It will be the beginning of finding a less stressful lifestyle.

### *Keep a journal as you read it*

By a journal we do not mean anything too spiritual or learned, just a good notebook or an online blog. Make this something you value. We suggest, if you are to use a notebook, getting one with a good binding, a cover you have chosen with some care and pages it's a pleasure to write on. If you do a blog, we suggest you keep it private and name it something significant. As to what to write in it, we regularly suggest things to write about throughout the book, but you may also want to write down encouraging words you have read or heard so that you can return to them. Do feel free to write your thoughts any time about anything that strikes you as you read – there is much value in writing like this. Your journal will become a kind of companion in your journey away from an overstressful life towards a more balanced one. It will stand as a permanent record you can return to to confer with as you journey. We hope you will win through to a better place after reading the book. If so, your journal will still be there as a reminder if you need it to help you avoid falling back into your old ways. The writing process itself is therapeutic; it helps us process our experience, organize our thoughts and be reconciled to our stress.

### *Consider having a spiritual accompanier help you through this particularly stressful time*

This person's role would be to listen to you, reflect back your thoughts and offer you reflections of his or her own for you to consider. If this is a new idea to you, be assured it is a centuries-old tradition, until recently more commonly called spiritual direction. Most denominations have networks for spiritual accompanying, with a coordinator who can put you in touch with one. Normally there are either no or only nominal charges. The time commitment is usually quite manageable – 90 minutes or so every six weeks. It is often best for your accompanier to be a stranger to you and not part of your life in any other way. This allows the accompanier to work free of other connotations and allows you to receive his or her guidance in the same way. One of the most common and difficult things about overstress is that it makes us feel isolated. We have often cut out of our lives things that have otherwise brought us companionship in order to cope with what is stressing us. Also, the general feeling of being down that we get when we are overstressed tends to make us avoid other people. So it's good to have this human link with another person as you start your journey.

# Part 1

# STRESS

# 1

# *What is stress?*

────── ◆●◆ ──────

## *Problem*

People in today's society seem to be suffering from an epidemic of stress. Almost every day we hear through the media of celebrities or sportspeople succumbing to it, or of surveys showing how stressed we are and how much time is lost at work because of stress-related illnesses. We all know of friends or relations who have said (or have said ourselves): 'I'm too stressed, I can't cope with all this pressure.' No one seems to be immune and for some the pressure becomes so great that they totally collapse or burn out.

Stress is frequently seen as a very unpleasant experience. We feel distressed by it. We chafe at feeling the way we do but it is difficult to escape from and not something we can easily switch out of. This is because these feelings of discomfort and tension arise from certain chemicals called stress hormones being pumped round our bodies in our blood, largely the hormone noradrenaline. The chemicals are released from glands into our bloodstream whenever we perceive (consciously or unconsciously) a demand – a need to perform better or a threat to us. So this might happen if we are meeting someone we love, are asked to squeeze an extra job into a busy schedule, run across a road to avoid traffic or go on a ride in a funfair. Equally the same reaction takes place if we suddenly confront a bull and need to run very fast. So both enjoyable and difficult situations trigger the same release of chemicals.

### Good stress

Our bodies are designed to cope with stress. The chemicals have a useful purpose and prepare our bodies to be more efficient and effective. They affect all the organs in our body, diverting blood to our muscles so that we are 'ready for action'. Blood is diverted from our guts and skin to our brain, heart and limb muscles, and we might feel 'sick with nerves' or the colour might drain from us and we go 'pale with fright' as a result of the blood being diverted. Our heart may feel as though it is racing as blood is pumped round more quickly to get glucose to our muscles, and we breathe more rapidly. Our eyes open wider and the pupil gets bigger so we can see more clearly. This is often called the 'fight or flight reaction' and is a primitive inbuilt response to perceived danger, which was necessary and very useful in the past when we were hunters, and would help us to be at our peak to deal with danger. The adrenaline triggers the release of another hormone called cortisol that helps us cope with stress by boosting our immune system and raising our energy levels.

Once the perceived threat has passed the hormones ebb away and we may then 'shake like a leaf' or complain that 'our legs feel like jelly' or 'our guts have turned to water'. This is the result of the adrenaline rush being over. Then we gradually relax and recover.

The world in which we live is very different now but the way our bodies respond to stress hasn't changed. So what happens to all that raw energy released into our system? We rarely have the opportunity actually to fight or run away in an ordinary day. We are more likely to knuckle down under pressure, hide our emotions and get on with the day. But the adrenaline still courses round our system and isn't dissipated so easily. Our muscles then feel tense and it may take a long time to calm down. I, Elizabeth, once had to sit a Spanish exam. All was going well until the adjudicator announced only five minutes to go. I was in the middle of copying a story I had written in rough, and as I raced to get it down on the paper before time was called, I felt my breathing get more rapid, my heart pounding as I was full of feelings of panic, anger at myself for mistiming things, and frustration. I sat at my desk writing as quickly as I could. The exam ended, but what surprised me was that my body didn't calm down straight away. I still felt tense and agitated after the exam, as I drove home and even for about another hour after I arrived home. I simply found it incredibly difficult to relax.

## Bad stress

When we hear people complaining of stress they are not usually referring to this inbuilt stress reaction to perceived danger. They are talking about the effects of prolonged stress.

So what has gone wrong? Crucially, the normal ebb and flow of hormones has been disrupted. For whatever reason, after a release of stress hormones we are not able to take adequate recovery time, we do not manage to get back to our resting state, but instead the stress hormones continue to course round our body making us feel very uncomfortable indeed. We may have so much to do that we cannot properly relax and recuperate, and we make demands on our bodies to keep on going. This is not a problem in the short term as eventually we will stop and rest and have some recovery time. However, if more and more demands pile in and we cut out our times of rest and relaxation in order to do everything demanded of us, our stress hormones never return to their resting state but stay abnormally high. As we have seen, stress hormones affect all our body systems, and we notice that we are always tense and on edge. We are overstressed. More noradrenaline gets pumped out, more cortisol is released and we begin to feel terrible. Eventually, when the body's stores of these hormones become depleted we may reach a state of ill health and even total collapse or burnout.

Angela described various times in her life when she had felt stressed and overwhelmed by what life was throwing at her. She particularly recalled the time her parents split up, when she was so worried that sleep was difficult and she wanted to run away and hide until it was all over. When she was taking university exams and deadlines loomed she found her brain wouldn't switch off and yet it was very difficult to concentrate and do useful work, and when her mother was in hospital she had to rush from one thing to another to fit in visiting, and barely had time to eat properly. Although she tried to carry on as normal with her church and working commitments, she felt that she gave less time for God when she should have been relying more on him. However, she says that when she did pray, her prayers were more heartfelt as she cried out to God.

People often tried to be helpful and wanted to fix her problems, when she would have preferred to be listened to. What really helped her, and still does, were times of rest, reflection and solitude.

Angela's advice to Christians suffering with stress is to be prepared to delegate and allow others to take over jobs you normally do, and to give yourself times of rest, to relax and reflect. This will prevent you from becoming more ragged and stressed.

## *Opportunity*

### Breathing exercise

If you are feeling stressed and finding it difficult to unwind and relax you can begin to do something about it now. One of the consequences of the stress chemicals in our bodies is to make our breathing rapid and shallow. By concentrating on our breathing we can begin to change this. Take some time to notice how you are breathing. Normally we are completely unaware of how we breathe; we only notice when breathing is difficult or we have a bad cough. So think about it. Now try breathing in deeply and slowly. Make sure that you are comfortable either sitting or lying down, and loosen any tight clothing you are wearing.

Fill up the whole of your lungs with air from the bottom to the top. Breathe in through your nose. Put your hand on your stomach and breathe in until you feel your stomach pushing out. This called diaphragmatic breathing, filling your lungs to their full capacity with air. Then breathe out deeply through your mouth, gently pushing all the air out of your lungs – your stomach will push in too. Repeat this deep breathing for several minutes, breathing in slowly and counting from one to five and breathing out slowly counting from one to five. Regular relaxed breathing practised for a few minutes two or three times a day helps you to feel calm, and is to do with the balance of chemicals in our bodies. It is also something you will be able to do at times in the day when you are feeling stressed.

## *Inspiration*

Joel Gascoigne writes a blog called buffer.com.[1] In May 2014 the following appeared:

[Recently] I religiously tried to follow a new routine I created for myself: a 7 day work week routine.

The idea was quite simple: I would work 7 days a week, rest 7 days a week, go to the gym 7 days a week, reflect 7 days a week. This was less about working lots, much more about feeling fulfilled every day, feeling stretched during the day but also rested. I aimed to work less each day, and replace two hours of work with a long break in the middle of the day . . .

I wanted every day to be exactly the same. So I worked each day, and rested each day. I went to the gym every day, I adjusted my work out so that this would be sustainable . . .

Overall, I feel like the 7 day work week fell apart because of lack of an extended period of renewal. My hypothesis that a couple of extra hours during the day and less overall daily hours working would be enough was invalidated in my experience.

After trying a 7 day work week, I became quite fascinated by the concept of a 'day of rest'. It occurred to me that this is a tradition that has been around for a very long time, and of separate origins. Almost all the world observes some form of a weekly 'day of rest'.

I'm no expert on the bible, however with a little research I found that the origin of the 'seventh day' or Sabbath is Genesis 2:2–3:

'And on the seventh day God ended His work which He had made; and He rested on the seventh day from all His work which He had made.'

Similarly, in Buddhism there is the concept of Uposatha, which is the Buddhist day of observance. I find it interesting how Buddhism teaches the purpose of this day:

'The cleansing of the defiled mind.'

I feel a sense of calm and confidence in the knowledge that many thousands of years of wisdom all converges towards the idea of a weekly day of rest. Certainly from my naive experiment I now feel that this is a very good practice.

Both from my own experiment and the wisdom of the day of rest, I have become interested in the idea of a single day of rest.

However, I have not once come across anything advocating two days of rest. This is one of my biggest takeaways from this experiment, and I plan to continue to work on the basis of 6 days of work and a single day of rest.

He received many comments on this blog, most from people saying they too had burned out when trying to work seven-day weeks and just became less efficient.

## *Meditation: Mark 2.27, 'The Sabbath was made for man, not man for the Sabbath'*

When we read the creation story in Genesis we are told that on the seventh day God had finished his work and rested from all the creative work he had done (Genesis 2.2–3). He made this day holy and different, and later when the Ten Commandments were given, the fourth commandment reminds us to keep a 'Sabbath' when we and our households rest and can be refreshed from our work (Exodus 20.8; 23.12). The Pharisees took this to extremes and made numerous rules about what did and did not constitute work. In the Gospels Jesus rebukes them and points out that the Sabbath was made for humankind, not given so that we would be burdened by rules. He is unafraid to do good and heals people on the Sabbath.

What are we to learn from this? First, that God built in a cyclical pattern of work and then rest for our well-being and refreshment. We ignore this at our peril. For our health's sake we need time to wind down from the stresses and strains of life.

Second, in Ezekiel 20.12 God says he gave the Sabbath as a sign so that the Israelites would know the Lord had made them holy. It is a regular reminder that we do not become holy by 'doing lots of good things'; it is a gift of grace, and God gives us time to 'just be' if we are prepared to take it. Our regular public worship is there to remind us also that by grace and faith we enter God's rest (Hebrews 4.2–3).

The problem for all of us is that we wrestle with this, wanting to earn God's favour, and find it very difficult to refrain from working every day. Like the Pharisees, we wonder what is work? In the ancient world and even until the machine age, people did heavy manual labour, and a day of rest would be a day of physical rest. In our modern world we may spend very little time doing physical work on a day-to-day basis, but lots of mental work (depending on our job and circumstance), and a day of rest may need to include physical things like sport, chopping logs or housework, and to rest and refrain from looking at work emails. The physical labour may be very recreative and refreshing. Perhaps a good rule of thumb is to have weekly time to do what refreshes us, what we find recreative, and also to join with others in worship.

## *Stressbuster: exercise*

Take some regular exercise. It is easy to stop exercising when you are pressed for time. It may be that you exercise already, like John, who enjoyed playing squash once a week and felt that hitting the ball really helped de-stress him. Or perhaps you are more like Sue who decided to walk each lunch hour for ten minutes, not too vigorously, window shopping or enjoying the gardens around, enough to switch her off from her desk work. Exercise is good for every level of our being and is a known de-stressor. It disperses the adrenaline we carry around with us, releases endorphins that improve our mood and helps to keep us healthy. Think of some exercise you could do regularly. You may prefer to cycle, run, swim or do Zumba. Start small and build up to more. Choose something you enjoy and will be able to keep up. Ryan joined a five-a-side football team and valued the camaraderie as well as the commitment, and noticed that he was feeling less stressed as a result.

# 2

# *How do I know if I'm overstressed?*

————•◦•◦•————

## *Problem*

It can be difficult to tell if we are overstressed, particularly if we've been exposed over a long period of time to events that make us feel stressed. Although we think we are giving ourselves adequate downtime for our hormone levels to get back to normal, that may not actually be the case. It does take time for the stress hormones to get back to a proper resting state and we may be the kind of people who find relaxing a challenge – or events overtake us and we have no alternative but to respond. Before we realize it we are living with our 'resting state' gradually rising. We never entirely wind down but are normally a bit taut. We constantly have stress hormones in our blood. We may feel on edge but a tipping point comes when we flip out over some seemingly minor event. We 'lose it' with our children or loved one, or we burst into tears at the slightest thing.

Our bodies are built to respond to short-term stress, and long-term stress has detrimental effects on both our physical and emotional health.

Grace worked for a large Christian organization. In her 50s, she was responsible for moving the organization's HQ from one country to another. At the same time she was coordinating an international conference of 150 delegates. She felt overwhelmed and stretched beyond her limits. Everything seemed to be a struggle. She worried that the event would descend into chaos and that she would let her team down. She was sleeping badly, lying awake at night with thoughts tossing around violently in her mind. At times she felt as if she was being smothered with a dark blanket – unable to see the way ahead and feeling helpless and constrained. Although she had some sense of God upholding her in all this, she also was filled with a sense of dread and foreboding, as if she was about to fall off a cliff. She found herself unable to concentrate and apply herself to her work.

Grace took some time off, but felt guilty about letting her colleagues down. She wanted to withdraw from people and spend time alone – to rest and escape from the burden of her responsibilities. After a period of rest she was able to get back to work. Her colleagues were very supportive and understanding, rather than feeling she had let them down. She says she has learnt to listen to her heart and body, to accept her limits and recognize the signs of burnout. Her perspective needed to change.

## Physical problems

Just as the stress hormones prepare many different systems in our bodies for action, as we saw in the last chapter, prolonged exposure to them can cause physical problems in many different areas. Stress hormones divert blood from the digestive system and the skin to the heart, brain and muscles. Chronically raised levels therefore are often associated with digestive or skin problems. This can include mild indigestion, stomach ulcers (as excess alcohol and smoking are often used to help us relax) and can be related to IBS (irritable bowel syndrome). People with poor circulation may notice their symptoms getting worse, or skin problems like psoriasis or eczema may flare up.

The effects on the heart and blood vessels can be more serious, causing raised blood pressure, chest pain and possible angina or irregular heartbeats. Muscle pain and tension headaches are linked to the high levels of stress hormones and the way we hold our muscles tensed for action.

The cumulative effect of chronic stress over time affects our immune system by depleting levels of the hormone cortisol, and we may succumb to repeated infections and minor illnesses, and generally feel very run down. We may be tempted to blame our stress on our run-down state, but it is probably the other way round.

## Emotional problems

When we are living only just within our capacity to cope, seemingly small events can trigger emotions that overwhelm us and make us feel out of control. So we lose our temper, burst into tears, feel anxious and panicky. These kinds of reactions tell us all is not well. Too much chronic stress makes us less able to cope with daily stresses and often produces a lot of negative feelings. Normally if something triggers a surge of emotion in a working day we have to suppress these feelings rather than cope with them as they occur, and we deal with them later. We can't just 'sound off' at work or church or with young children. We suppress our feelings, deal with the issue and carry on. When we stop to unwind we find those feelings resurfacing and have time to reflect on and deal with them. The problem with being chronically overstressed is that there is never time to deal with the bad feelings and they hang around as a constant backcloth to life and may affect the way we think, affecting our ability to concentrate or to make sound judgements. We lose our sense of proportion and humour, are generally more irritable and may become cynical. We feel emotionally exhausted and, although we can generally keep up appearances, more detached and less emotionally connected to people. Perhaps we function on autopilot. Our sense of joy and wonder in life disappears.

## Sleep problems

A major factor that compounds all of this is that overstress often leads to poorer sleep and that in turn makes us feel fatigued and unable to deal efficiently with our life. Sleep not only rests our bodies but also seems to enable our brains to process what has happened to us through the day. When we are asleep our blood pressure falls and so do the levels of some stress hormones. Unfortunately when we are overstressed we often sleep less well, either finding it difficult to drop off to sleep or waking through the night and lying awake churning problems over.

So if you are reading this and thinking 'That's me' or beginning to realize that your repeated bouts of minor illness are telling you that you are overstressed, it's time to think hard about doing something to escape this vicious cycle before you become completely exhausted and collapse.

## *Opportunity*

Here is a checklist to look at and consider whether or not you are living in a state of overstress. It is taken from our book *The Essential Guide to Burnout*.[1] It would be good for you to use your journal to reflect on this list and measure your own stress levels from it. And then, maybe, to discuss your findings with your spiritual accompanier afterwards.

### Changes in behaviour
*Working harder and longer but achieving less*
Have you been putting in longer hours? Have you been working at home more? Have you been feeling you are not keeping up with things at work as well as you would like? Does it take you longer to work through tasks? Is it harder to keep a sense of proportion about your workload? Are you getting less satisfied with your working outcomes? Are you clock watching? Are you being late (both arriving and leaving)? Are you losing your creative problem-solving ability?

*An inability to pursue recreational and recovery needs*
Have you become so absorbed in work that you have cut down your social life? Have you picked up from those around that you are getting boring? When did you last have a good evening out? Have you found it difficult to forget about work? How do you spend time off – is it largely just vegging out? Do you feel you have to cram the ordinary things of life (shopping, cleaning, cooking and so on) into too little space? A recent study suggested that thinking about work during leisure time and getting less than six hours sleep a night are key factors for subsequent burnout.

*Using mood-altering drugs to help cope with the increased demand*
Have you, in order to keep going under great pressure, increased the amount of caffeine and/or alcohol you drink? Are you using recreational drugs? Do you smoke more? Are you binging or eating fast food more? Has internet porn become a problem? Do you find you are craving treats more to lift your mood?

### Changes in feelings
*When we are on the verge of burnout we feel different from normal*
Have you lost your sense of humour? Have you become resentful more of the time? Have you a feeling of powerlessness? Do you persistently feel a sense of failure? Do you feel guilty about things not going well? Do you feel responsible all the time? Have you been more irritable at work and at home? Have you had flashes of anger? Have you 'lost it' with anyone recently?

### Changes in thinking
*As well as feeling different from normal, when we are on the edge of burnout we have changes in our thinking*
Have you had increasing thoughts of leaving your job? Has it been increasingly difficult to concentrate? Are you more cautious and suspicious about things? Have you become at all cynical, expecting things not to turn out well? Have you developed a victim mentality in any way? Are you preoccupied with your own needs and personal survival, rather than the bigger picture?

### Changes in health
*Overstress affects our health, causing physical problems, especially in wearing down our immune system*
Have you been getting frequent minor illnesses? Have you become more susceptible to infections, coughs and colds? Do you feel weary and tired all day? Has your sleep pattern become disordered? Have you had any digestive disorders? Have you had any skin disorders, especially psoriasis? Are you chronically tired and listless? Have you any emotional/mental health issues? Are you susceptible to unaccountable weeping fits or mood swings? Have you been suffering from insomnia?

Use this opportunity to take stock of what is happening to you. Count how many of the questions you have been able to answer 'yes' to. If you have answered 'yes' to a number of them you are definitely showing signs and symptoms of overstress. Don't rush past it and on to the next thing. If you are showing signs and symptoms of overstress, note it and decide to do something about it, however small. 'The origin of stress may sometimes lie outside ourselves, but its treatment is always inside us.'[2] It may be that in the short term you are only able to change something very small. It is often the 'straw that breaks the camel's back'. Is there a very small change to your life you could make immediately that would ease a little of the pressure, even if only for a short while? It may be something like switching your phone off for half an hour while you eat your evening meal, taking five minutes in the day to yourself, reading a magazine or leaving work on time once a week. Decide to make one small but manageable change in the next few weeks, but also plan to take time to think about a longer-term solution. This would be something to note in your journal or discuss with your spiritual accompanier or a good friend.

## *Inspiration*

Paul was a teacher in a comprehensive school in a deprived area. He was a special educational needs coordinator (SENCO) and under a great deal of stress, dealing with the problems and difficulties of many needy and disadvantaged pupils. He was coming up to retirement age and would have liked to retire early but was unable to because his family needed his income. He recognized within himself several of the changes overstress brings and was afraid he would break down completely, but didn't see a way out of his situation. It was suggested to him that he change one small thing – that he take five minutes each day simply to sit quietly with God, not praying or reading, just being. Initially he replied that it would be impossible – he simply didn't have a spare minute in the day. Then he decided to sit quietly in his car when he arrived at work. Instead of getting out as soon as he arrived and dashing early into school to prepare for the day, he took five minutes to be still with God.

This very small change produced astonishing results. His attitude began to change and he was able to work until he retired, and then to do some supply teaching that he enjoyed. He introduced a second five minutes of stillness in the middle of the day, his 'Jesus time'. So important did it become in sustaining him that he maintained it throughout the rest of his life, even when he suffered from a debilitating terminal illness.

## *Meditation: 1 Kings 17–19, 21*

Elijah was a fighter and a firm believer in God. He was not afraid to be unpopular and speak the unpalatable truth to the king, even if it was dangerous. He lived on the edge. He was a man under lots of stress. After telling Ahab that there would be a drought (by implication because Ahab had disregarded God), he goes into hiding as he knows he is on a hit list. At these difficult times in his life he experiences God's remarkable provision for him – the ravens (1 Kings 17.4–6); the widow (1 Kings 17.7–14). He is a man with a lot of faith, and he sees his prayers answered – raising the widow's son (1 Kings 17.22–24).

He is bold and tuned into God, and a couple of years later he again confronts Ahab with his faults. Then there is a psychological battle with the prophets of Baal and a very public display of faith in the true God on Mount Carmel. What a powerful and emotive day that was when God rained down fire on Elijah's sacrifice! When Ahab and the people drift back down the mountain, Elijah climbs to the top of it and wrestles in prayer for rain. Seven times he sends his servant to look for rain clouds before the cloud 'as small as a man's hand' is spotted by the sea. He doesn't give up easily. After all this he doesn't take rest. Elijah sprints ahead of Ahab's chariot all the way to Jezreel (about 15 miles). He may have hoped that the wonderful display of God's sovereignty on Mount Carmel would cause Jezebel, Ahab's wife, to repent. However, she is enraged by what had happened to the priests of Baal, and makes a death threat against Elijah. He runs for his life to Beersheba, about 100 miles away, to get as far from Jezebel as he can! He then journeys into the desert for a day before sitting down in some shade and praying that he might die. He has had no time to wind down and recover from the physical and emotional stress he has been under, and it affects his mood and thinking. What has happened to his faith? His life today doesn't seem worth living, but only shortly before he had had a truly mountain-top experience of God acting in power. His physical strength is drained too, and he is told by angels to eat, drink and rest and then to journey to a safe place (Mount Horeb) and hide in a cave.

While there he meets God in the 'still small voice', not in the powerful displays of wind, earthquake and fire, a reminder perhaps not to keep on pushing himself but to be 'quiet ' in every sense, and to rest.

Elijah is an example of how even the most committed and faithful believers can get overstressed and exhausted doing God's work, to a point where their emotional and physical health can suffer. Elijah's thinking changed as a result of overstress. His sense of proportion disappeared, as did his sense of purpose. Gone was his ability to believe God was in control and he gave up, wanting to die and feeling his life was pointless and not worthwhile. God, however, is working on a much bigger scale, and Elijah's ups and downs fit into a bigger pattern. It is worth our remembering this too in all the strains and stresses of our lives. It is all too easy to get caught up in the immediate and to fail to remember that actually God is in control, but that he is working on a much broader canvas and sees the whole picture. At the end of the story Elijah goes on to have a significant, if less flamboyant role to play, and he witnesses Ahab's repentance and turning back to God.

## Stressbuster: the outdoors

One small thing you may be able to do is to get outdoors, daily, for however short a time. Even in a busy city life, take time to get in the fresh air. Notice natural things. It's surprisingly profound and feeds our hungry soul. This evening, going for a short walk in winter, we saw the most amazingly vivid sunset, turning the sky every shade of red, pink and orange and simply lifting the heart. You may hear birdsong, children playing, see an isolated flower, star or tiny crescent moon. Take a moment to notice. Being absorbed however briefly with natural things lowers the blood pressure and is de-stressing. It is all too easy to rush from house to car or bus and be thinking of work or worries and not notice what is around and freely available.

# 3

## *I know I'm overstressed but how do I stop?*

### *Problem*

Having read the first two chapters you may have found that they were describing your situation and you've had to admit to yourself that you really are overstressed. Perhaps you have physical or emotional symptoms of chronic stress and now understand what is contributing to them. Or you may have known you were under prolonged stress for some time but have not felt able to admit to it or do anything about it. There are several reasons why we don't act to reduce our stress even when we know in some part of ourselves how detrimental it is to our health and sense of well-being.

*First, it may not be practical for us to reduce our workload or other commitments* because others are depending on us. We may want to stop our work but have a mortgage or rent to pay, or elderly relatives or young children needing us to help with their care. We may have committed to do something in our community or church and now feel we cannot pull out – that we need to honour our word. So we feel hemmed in by outer circumstances, wanting something to change but unable to sort it out. We may not be able to change things but as we will see later in the chapter, there may be small changes we can make that will help alleviate our stress levels.

*Second, we can be hemmed in by our understanding of God.* We may have a belief that denying ourselves is what God wants; after all, isn't that written in the Gospel (Matthew 16.24)? As Christians our desire is to work hard for God, living out our lives for him. Within the church we wish to be seen as committed, and take as our role models Christians we admire or Bible figures. Perhaps we read biographies of Christians around the world and want in some small way to emulate them. Usually such people are passionate, courageous, faithful and devoted. They are not normally characterized as having a balanced life. We too want to give of ourselves selflessly to please God. All of this is good.

We may feel that all of our lives should be working for God and that it is self-indulgent to care for ourselves when there are so many unmet needs around us. We find it hard or impossible to say 'no' when demands are made of us because to do so would appear selfish. Besides, we may think that God will sort it all out if we commit to him what we are doing, and we should just trust him. But this kind of thinking has many pitfalls and is based on some underlying false beliefs.

*Third, our 'drivenness' is perhaps a result of our upbringing* and has been the lens through which we have approached our Christian life, and may have distorted the truth. If we have been raised in a family where working hard and being successful is very important, we unconsciously adopt that view of life from a very early age. Words like 'must', 'ought' and 'should' are usually words learnt from our parents, and as we grow older we can attribute them to God. The idea that we should be working all of our waking hours is not God's, and our busyness can be due to family patterns rather than an emblem of our commitment to God. Are we really sure that within our punishing lifestyle we prioritize what God wants us to prioritize in life?

*Fourth, we may have the type of personality that enjoys the buzz that comes from living under pressure.* Are we on a treadmill of our own making, addicted to the adrenalin produced by stress and pressure? In his book *The Addiction of a Busy Life*, Edward England writes about his realization that he was hooked on being busy and having tight deadlines.[1] Certain personality types (type A) are more prone to this than others and enjoy the adrenalin produced by living to deadlines, driving themselves hard and pushing themselves on all sorts of fronts to achieve. That is the case for many young men and women working in the finance industry, who drive themselves to the limits of physical and mental endurance in their punishing schedules. If that's you, it may be very hard to let go of all the activity because you are used to having lots of adrenalin pumping round your system making you feel more alive. However, ultimately living that sort of lifestyle has serious physical and emotional consequences, as we have seen in the previous chapter.

God speaks to us through our bodies. If our bodies are complaining that they are exhausted, God is saying something to us that we shouldn't ignore. Maybe this is a new idea to us. We are used to God speaking through the sermon, the Bible or maybe a good friend, but we are often adept at ignoring our bodies, denying what our weary limbs or mind are trying to say to us.

## *Opportunity*

If we can begin to understand and know ourselves, what makes us tick and where our strengths and weaknesses lie, we may be able to begin to redress the balance in our lives. We need to acknowledge that people are all built differently and to try and understand our own strengths and pressure points, not comparing ourselves with others. In *The Essential Guide to Burnout* we write:

> Burnout is linked to two types of personality [though it can happen to anyone], both with the kind of qualities professional people are expected to show. Both of these have admirable elements but, as we shall see, if they are not balanced with other things, they can lead to burnout. The two types of personality are:
> - people who are conscientious, hard-working, and highly motivated with drive and commitment
> - people with high levels of compassion and concern for others, who have high ideals and are willing to sacrifice self in order to help others.[2]

Often Christian people have or aspire to have these characteristics.

There are many ways to try and deepen our understanding of ourselves. We may try and talk seriously with a close friend. This is only helpful if we truly listen and take on board what they are saying to us! Or we may want to talk some of these things through with our spiritual accompanier. We can journal about them as we recommend in our introduction to this book.

We may want to use or look again at a widely used personality indicator such as the Myers Briggs Type Indicator (see the Resources section at the end of this book). This is often used in work and church situations and may begin to help us understand our personality preferences and also suggest ways to relax.

Or we may want to meet with a counsellor or therapist to look at how we have been influenced by our upbringing in ways that are unhelpful and do not encourage a sustainable, creative and balanced life.

Western society is left-brain dominated, our value as people being measured by what we do and achieve. Ruth Fowke writes 'I sometimes pick up the impression that many stressed-out people think that the Creator God is only interested in their left brain hemisphere and that He probably regrets making the other half!'[3] Why do we assume that God is only interested in the left side of our brain? That is the side that is analytical and does things sequentially in order. The right side of the brain is more spatially aware and is associated with the creative, the imaginative and the artistic. These right-brain activities are what many people relegate to leisure time only and are often the first to go under stress. But this is the side of our brain that nourishes us as people. We deny using it at our peril. Maybe we need to give ourselves permission to spend time being more creative and artistic and playful. Jot down in your journal any thoughts you have about this.

## *Inspiration*

Edward England, mentioned earlier, was a former director of the publisher Hodder & Stoughton. He was responsible for launching the NIV Bible in Britain and also edited the magazine *Renewal* for ten years. He relished being busy, starting new projects at work. His story is not so very different from those of the many successful and competitive young men and women in today's professions. He attended a busy church and took on many responsibilities there, as well as being on the board of several major organizations. On holiday one day he realized he was 'addicted to a busy life', and he was somewhat miffed to have to see himself like this rather than as an 'actively committed' Christian. The former tag has a negative connotation but the latter is viewed highly in Christian circles. He seemed to need the adrenaline buzz, which is what kept him so busy.

Despite this insight it took a mild, and then later a major heart attack, which put him in hospital, before he really had to confront his addiction and do something about it.

In doing so, while convalescing he learnt many lessons and wrote a book to amplify them – *The Addiction of a Busy Life*. His circumstances brought him to a full stop in hospital, but he writes openly about the difficulties of knowing how to pace himself in the future and not to slip into being as busy again. He ends the book, while waiting for a possible pacemaker for his heart, with a prayer for God to be his pacemaker in the day-to-day decisions of life. Perhaps this is a prayer you can make.

As I plan my day, the weeks ahead, and consider the appointments in my diary:
*Heavenly Father be my pacemaker.*

As the demands of life thrust themselves upon me, the duties, the responsibilities from which I should not hide:
*Heavenly Father be my pacemaker.*

When I am sometimes frail, unable to cope with people's expectations:
*Heavenly Father be my pacemaker.*

When my urge is to respond to any challenge, still me and be my peace.
Show me what I should and shouldn't do.
When I run ahead of you, or drop behind, bring me into step, that I may rest my tent where yours is.
God of action, God of stillness, God of peace; who asks us to bear our burdens and to lay them down, activate and deactivate me, that I may respond only to your command.
When the hardest thing is to pause when I wish to press ahead, to accept your rhythm when I see constant opportunities, may my heart beat in time with yours.
*Heavenly Father be my pacemaker.*[4]

## Meditation: Matthew 25.12–30

The Scriptures speak of using all of our talents for God and of being good stewards of the resources God has given us. God wants us to use what he has given us and not to 'bury' or hide away and ignore some of our talents. God has given each of us a body, mind and soul. Not everyone is the same and some have more physical or mental stamina and abilities than others. He has made all of us as whole people, each one in his image, which means we are all creative and playful as well as rational beings. To know what gifts and talents we have means that we need to know ourselves. We cannot love ourselves if we do not know who we are and what talents we have, and we are told to love others as we love ourselves (Matthew 19.19). We can make the mistake of trying to love others and not loving ourselves.

Realizing that we are trapped in a narrow lifestyle of overwork is the first step to change. We may need to give ourselves permission to stop and relax, viewing it as good stewardship of our resources. If we think of it this way, rather than as an indulgence, we may achieve a better life balance and be able to 'serve the Lord with gladness' rather than eventually grinding to a halt. In some measure it is a change of mindset that is needed. If we are very overcommitted, maybe there is one small change we can make in the short term, but we need also to consider a long-term solution.

It may be helpful to ask whether we are living using only one half of our brain most of the time. Do we filter out the opportunities for play, leisure and creativity because we are too busy doing 'important' or 'urgent' things? If so we should not be surprised when we become unwell, because we are only living half a life. We have a supply of untapped resources even within us, all those right-brain activities we are putting on hold because of busyness. When thought of like this, using only half our resources is ridiculous and also like burying our talents and hiding them away. God wants us to glorify him by living as whole people, not those who ignore or give no expression to our creativity. And if we do not take time to play, relax and recover, we are setting ourselves on a course that may well end in serious ill health.

Then we may find we are unable to do any of the things we have devoted our life to. The colloquial expression 'It's no use flogging a dead horse' is all the more poignant when we read Robert Murray M'Cheyne's words about himself, spoken as he lay dying. He was a devoted Christian minister who first systematized Bible reading and came up with a Bible-reading plan, but he died at the young age of 29. On his deathbed he said to a friend: 'God gave me a message to deliver and a horse to ride. Alas I have killed the horse and now I cannot deliver the message.'[5]

## *Stressbuster: taking breaks*

Do you find it hard to take breaks? Are you the sort of person who still keeps working through coffee and lunch breaks? Decide that you are going to take proper breaks. Studies have shown that people work more efficiently if they take regular breaks. Take a lunch break. Guard your evenings and weekends. Take all your entitled holidays and plan them well ahead. Do all you can to stop work invading your personal time.

Sarah became very run down and exhausted through working regular long hours over and above her committed work time. Her children said that she could only talk about work. When she began to suffer from stress-related illness she at last took notice of her loved ones and stopped bringing work home to do. She turned her work mobile off overnight and left it at home on holiday. At first she felt guilty, but as she began to feel better in herself, she noticed she was getting through all her work anyway, and she was enjoying giving her children quality time. Her children found her much more fun to be with.

*Part 2*

# GOD

# 4

# *How can I make time for God?*

## *Problem*

This chapter is about looking at our personal devotional time. The next chapter looks more closely at what we believe. When we are under a lot of stress it unavoidably affects all our relationships, and our relationship with God is no exception.

Many Christians have been taught the importance of making time each day for God as a way to build up a relationship with him. They would be taught to take some 'quiet time' for prayer and Bible reading each day, and given pointers on how to use this focused time. This was the norm for Christians of many different denominations not so long ago. In our pastoral experience we doubt that very many committed Christians today manage to keep to it. Even strongly connected Christians who are regular worshippers at church seem to pray on the hoof – as they are walking the dog or driving the car – rather than have a quiet period each day. When they do read the Bible it may be using Bible notes that look at a particular verse, and not often a more meaty study of doctrinal issues. Many only read the New Testament and have only a hazy knowledge of what the Old Testament writers are saying. As with all relationships, if we give little time to them they become more distant.

### Too busy

There have been several times in my life when God has had to take a back seat because of other pressures. When I was a junior doctor I had to work long hours on call as well as a nine-to-five day on the wards. Usually the last thing I felt like doing when I had some time to myself was to try and have a quiet time with God. I wanted to sleep, eat or just watch TV. The same thing happened when I had very young children. At first I would try to get up early before they woke to try and pray and read my Bible. Somehow my baby seemed to cotton on to that and simply woke up earlier too. The few minutes I felt I had to myself in a day were to do jobs, make meals or walk the dog. God seemed one thing too many to fit into my life. The books I read or tried to read on prayer had obviously been written by men with time on their hands, or so it seemed, and not women struggling with young children. There didn't seem to be any helpful advice for someone pressed for time and energy.

There can be many times in our lives when we are too busy and have lots of tasks or goals before us and get 'hurry sickness'. It may come from pressure at work, within our family situation or from friends. We hurry from one thing to another without a break, simply trying to fit everything in. Finding time to devote ourselves to prayer seems impossible and impractical. We simply cannot stop. Our devotions end up becoming a burden rather than a solace and a source of strength. God begins to seem very far away.

### Feeling guilty

However, if we have ever been in the practice of giving God time in our day and reading our Bibles regularly, such a change leaves us feeling very guilty. We know or have been taught how very important it is to cultivate our devotional life, and it is as if that whole area has gone wild and is in complete disorder. Our guilt makes it hard to try and approach God at all. The longer we avoid praying the more difficult it gets. We hide ourselves from God without really wanting to, pushing away or ignoring the prompts that come from within.

We look at other Christians around us and think we are very second-class citizens of heaven because we don't feel we are walking close to God at all. And worse than that, we don't have the time or energy to do anything about it.

This is a particular stress that Christians feel. Those of our non-Christian friends and colleagues who are under various kinds of stress may not have to cope with this particular added burden of guilt. They seem to have one less thing to fit into their life.

## Feeling a failure

We not only feel guilty, we also feel a failure. In our minds we are not living up to our own standards. We should be able to get ourselves organized into a more orderly lifestyle, or so we tell ourselves. We feel we are letting God down. We've allowed ourselves to be caught in a trap that we seem unable to get out of. And feeling such a failure, we don't talk about it or share our concerns with those close to us, or see clearly what is happening.

Going to church can become very painful, as sermons, hymns and songs exhort us to high standards in our Christian life. We perhaps resolve to do better in the coming week, but if we then don't manage to we are again in the vicious cycle of failure and guilt. We may want to stop going to church so often because we know we'll end up feeling more guilty and more of a failure.

When we are coping with prolonged stress our thinking can change – we don't think clearly or rationally under stress. We are preoccupied with personal survival and don't think about the bigger picture. We may find our thinking is fuzzy and we lack concentration, or we become cynical and negative. We may feel 'What's the point in going to church or praying?' The feelings of guilt and failure can send us spiralling down into despair. We are hopeless Christians, so maybe God has given up on us too. Such thoughts are extremely stressful and difficult to cope with, on top of all the other pressures we are under; but as we shall see, God sees the bigger picture and is able to use our failures to help us grow closer to him.

# *Opportunity*

## New ways to pray

Instead of thinking there is no way forward, perhaps we could see our difficulties with prayer as an opportunity. Because of our pressurized circumstances we are not able to give God time the way we did in the past. Here is a chance to find a new way to live in God's presence that we are able to manage on a daily basis.

## Personality

In her book *Personality and Stress*, Ruth Fowke says that many Christians berate themselves for not 'praying in the right way' and can lose their joy. Her book is about how differing prayer styles suit different personality types, and contrasts the way 'thinkers' and 'feelers' prefer to pray. Feelers don't think they have prayed properly unless their feelings are stirred when they pray, whereas thinkers like to have 'understood something and gain insight'.[1] Understanding this can help us opt for the model of prayer that sits best with us. But it is important to remember that prayer is about being attentive to God, and doesn't depend on feelings or understanding.

## Perseverance

Another book that helped us was Margaret Hebblethwaite's *Motherhood and God*.[2] In it she writes: 'I had not prayed for years but it was like a little nag at the back of my conscience.' She goes on to describes how our own perception of being a parent can inform us about God's unconditional and unwavering love for us, and that we can learn from our children. When thinking of our repeated failings in prayer she remembers one of her children learning to crawl. Despite falling over, getting hurt and weeping, the child never gave up, kept on and on trying and failing and trying to crawl until at last it succeeded. She had looked on in wonder and surprise and delight at its doggedness, and soothed it when hurt. Surely, she says, a loving God takes pleasure in our bungling attempts to pray too.

## Pausing

One lovely idea we have tried – and often failed – to incorporate into our own lives is the practice of 'pausing'. We often go about our daily lives with ourselves closed off to God, through fear, fatigue or habit. We practise pausing by taking a deep breath and opening ourselves to God, before answering the phone, looking at emails, responding to a request, going through a door and many more times in the day. As you breathe, open yourself to God and pray for wisdom in the task ahead. When the task is finished, breathe deeply again and thank God for his presence. If we do this regularly our day will be punctuated with moments when we are consciously aware of God in the midst of our business, and we will be less driven by 'hurry sickness'. If this appeals to you, try it out for a day or two and see what difference it makes. If you start off well and then forget, don't worry – be like the child learning to crawl. Pick yourself up and try again! Talking this all through with a spiritual director or accompanier will be encouraging and helpful.

## *Inspiration*

In the seventeenth century a French Carmelite friar sought to know and love God in this way. His name was Brother Lawrence and he is known and famous for a little devotional book, *The Practice of the Presence of God*, a collection of letters he wrote to those around him. I had heard of this book over many years but always avoided it, thinking it would only make me feel more guilty than ever about what I was not managing to do. Recently I came across it and decided to read it, and had a lovely surprise. It is a very slim book, full of gentle and wise letters of encouragement to ordinary people in ordinary circumstances.

Brother Lawrence found that the set times of prayer in the monastic life were no different from other times of day for him; that he didn't feel nearer to God in focused prayer time than in daily life. He thought it was a great delusion to think that times of prayer should differ from other times. He worked in the kitchen of a Paris monastery and wrote that 'in the noise and clatter of my kitchen, while several people are together calling for as many different things, I possess God in as great tranquillity as when upon my knees at the Blessed Sacrament'.[3]

Reading this book it becomes clear that the word 'practice' is very important. A sense of God's presence with us all the time can only be obtained by the regular and repeated practice of offering what we are about to do to God and thanking him after we have done it. He recommends this practice to a soldier, saying 'No one will notice it, and nothing is easier than to repeat often in the day these little internal adorations.'[4]

He writes in a very down-to-earth way and is well aware of thoughts drifting off elsewhere. When that happened to him he simply turned his mind back to God again. His view was that when we repeatedly turn to God inwardly, in time this becomes a habit and then God's presence with us seems quite natural as we go about the day, and leads to an inner peace and centredness. His view was that the presence of God is reached by the heart and love rather than by our minds understanding – '*thoughts* count for little, *love* is everything'.[5]

## *Meditation*

Hanging in our porch we have a plaque bought from the bookshop at Canterbury Cathedral that reads 'Bidden or not bidden, God is present.' It serves as a reminder to us as we go in and out of the door that whether we are aware of it or not, God is present with us all the time, whatever we are doing. This is not a new idea and runs through Scripture in many places. We have picked out a couple of verses to meditate on more fully. The first is Psalm 89.15–16, which reads: 'Blessed are those who have learned to acclaim you, who walk in the light of your presence, LORD. They rejoice in your name all day long.' This delightful verse in the middle of the psalm reminds us that we can live our ordinary daily lives in God's presence, but it is something we need to learn to become aware of. It fits well with our thoughts of pausing and turning our hearts to God in the midst of our daily work and business.

The second verse is Romans 12.1, where Paul writes: 'I urge you, bothers and sisters, in view of God's mercy, to offer your bodies as a living sacrifice, holy and pleasing to God – this is your true and proper worship.'

William Barclay, in his commentary on Romans, writes: 'Paul says "take your body; take all the tasks that you have to do every day; take the ordinary work of the shop, the office, the factory . . . and offer all that as an act of worship to God." . . . *Real worship is the offering of everyday life to [God]*.'[6] If we can consider all our daily jobs and commitments as being part of our true worship of God, instead of something that gets in the way of our being able to worship God, this will free us from guilt and despair, and give new meaning to our everyday lives.

So as you think about your hectic daily life in which you feel you are struggling, be heartened and remember that God is close by, waiting for you to tune in to him at any moment, understanding that you have many tasks to do, that your mind is weary and that you will seek to offer him the love of your heart moment by moment as you pause, breathe him in, thank him and practise being aware of his presence.

## *Stressbuster: taking a deep breath*

'Stop, take a deep breath and count to ten.' I remember being told to do this as a child when I was feeling very angry. Somehow those brief moments of stopping helped steady the emotions and helped me to think clearly. Pausing can be like that, but more pleasurable, and helps to calm us and make us feel less driven.

Deliberately pause between things. Stop, take a deep breath and acknowledge God before entering a building, starting your car, eating a meal, answering the phone or email. It doesn't take long and doesn't look obvious. Break up the endless rush with a few moments' reflection, and see if you are not feeling calmer by the end of the day.

Lee tried 'pausing' after it was suggested by a colleague. He was sceptical at first but had to admit that he felt calmer and more in control. Instead of trying to do several things at once he found that pausing helped him focus more clearly on the task in hand. His mind wasn't darting off to the next thing he wanted to do.

Give it a try for 24 hours and see what you think.

# 5

## *How can I reconnect with God?*

---

### *Problem*

We suspect that in some cases another cumulative effect of all the stress factors looked at so far might well be a lack of confidence in our core beliefs as Christians. We may not only be finding it difficult to be Christians right now but also wondering if we even believe in Christianity any more, or as fully as in the past.

As with other elements of being a Christian, having absolute core beliefs is not fashionable in the modern culture. The plurality of the culture has made adherence to a particular set of values to the exclusion of others seem narrow and opinionated. People prefer to sit light and keep their options open. There is a reluctance to commit to a clearly defined set of values and join an organization that embraces them. An example of this in ordinary society would be the plummeting memberships of the political parties, which have suffered a worse numerical decline in the last 20 years than the churches.

Within the Church there has been a parallel turning away from emphasizing clear doctrinal teaching as a priority, so that the differences between where the Christian faith stops and something else begins are very blurry in the public perception. A *Church Times* interview with a Canadian atheist minister, Gretta Vosper, quotes her as saying:

> The role of an atheist minister is exactly the same as any other person in pastoral ministry, except that I'm also responsible for ensuring that anything which comes out of West Hill [my congregation within the United Church of Canada], as an official

document or presentation is devoid of exclusive theological language . . . We are very intentional about creating a theologically barrier-free space.[1]

We give this as an illustration of how the importance of holding a set of core beliefs has been radically downgraded both in the Church and in society at large – and notice the implication that a clear theological statement is going to be 'exclusive'. Firm beliefs have become a pejorative thing.

I, Andrew, once allowed and led a non-faith 'Time of celebration for the life of X', as we called it, in my church. It was for a very prominent and much-loved atheist member of our community who had died, and the church was the only place big enough to host the numbers coming. It went very well and I was pleased to work with and be guided by a friend of X's from the National Secular Society who regularly took non-faith funerals. Two things took me by surprise in the numerous conversations I held at the wake following. First, I was hugely popular. I couldn't get to the sandwiches for people accosting me warmly and thanking me, pleased that I had allowed it. Second, I was regularly told that 'It's all the same isn't it?' or 'It was like a funeral in all that matters.'

There had been no mention of Jesus Christ, his death, resurrection; the hope Christians have of eternal life; no prayers, Scripture, commendation to God; no Blessing. Yet to that gathering of several hundred informed, intelligent people it was all the same. I am quite sure that if I had decided otherwise and not allowed the event (and I did give it a lot of thought before allowing it), far from being popular I would have been thought uncaring and narrowly doctrinaire. This event seems to me to sum up where we are on matters of core belief in the current culture.

A further factor can be added to all this to see how an ordinary Christian with orthodox beliefs could begin to lose confidence in them. Within theological circles, for well over 150 years the prevailing culture has been one of questioning and doubt. There is serious doubt among many mainstream theologians of the historicity of Jesus, especially his teachings and his miracles. Many Old Testament scholars doubt whether any of the first five books of the Bible are historical.

They don't believe in the Genesis accounts of the patriarchs, the Exodus from Egypt or the conquest of the Promised Land, which doesn't leave a lot. Not all scholars hold these views but it is certainly true that many do, and that anyone undertaking any kind of theological training, even for local church work like local preaching in Methodism or readership in Anglicanism, let alone ordination, will be expected to look hard at these views and may well be taught by those who espouse them.

## *Opportunity*

If we are feeling somewhat unsure of our beliefs in Jesus, let it be an opportunity to look to those beliefs afresh. It might be some time since we did it. The best thing with doubt is always to take the bull by the horns and think what exactly it is we are doubting – then to work at this until we come to a clear conclusion about whether to abandon our belief or abandon any further doubting. Doubt thrives on vagueness. If we can get down to some sustained thought, then one way or another doubt has to go away. So here are some suggestions about engaging ways to readdress our core beliefs in Jesus.

First, we might like to sign up to a course on Christian belief. The Alpha course is the best known and is hugely successful. It is now so widespread that there will be several happening nearby wherever you are in the UK. It's also international. However, there are any number of good courses one might attend. We give contact details for Alpha course in the Resources section, as well as for some other courses. Going on a course has the advantage of our meeting with other course members and so sharing ideas and impressions and asking questions. Doubt often thrives on isolation, so for that reason too, a course is a good thing.

Second, we might read a good book on Christian basics. There are plenty of these. Again, we give our recommendations for this, covering a variety of styles of writing, in the Resources section.

Third, we might like to go on a retreat. In our ever more frantic culture, people of all faiths and none are finding the value of retreating to a place of quietness and sanctuary. There are many retreat centres around the country. They offer space in a peaceful environment to pray and be thoughtfully reflective. It's possible to go for just a few hours, up to several days or even weeks. Many centres offer guidance to retreatants, especially if retreating is new to them. Again, see the Resources section.

Fourth, we might like to go on a pilgrimage. There has been a recent revival of the medieval practise of pilgrimage – physically journeying to some place of spiritual importance. Pilgrimages can range from quite luxurious tours with hotel accommodation and coach travel to tough long-distance walking or cycling. Many Christians have found going on a pilgrimage to be an inspiring way to renew their belief in Jesus. Our daughter and son-in-law recently walked 100 kilometres of one of the most famous pilgrim routes, to Santiago de Compostela in northern Spain. They found it an amazing experience, not least for the great variety of people they met from many nationalities who were also walking. The different reasons they were walking were fascinating. It built up their faith.

Fifth, we might like to commit to some act of service. A woman in our present congregation has just gone out with a charity to Ghana to do community work there. The charity is not an especially Christian one but she is seeking, as well as to do some good there, to find God in a new way. Her blog is inspiring. God is often found among the poor and disadvantaged. If we commit to doing something to help them as part of our quest for a clearer, firmer faith, we may well find he meets us there. It's interesting that the doubting theological culture, mentioned above, is largely limited to the affluent countries. It gets no purchase in the poorer parts of the world, where you might think the deprivation would cause people to doubt God more readily. The voice of God is clearer to the poor and we might do well to join them for a time.

## Inspiration

When we are tempted to waver in our faith it is inspirational to consider those who believe so deeply that they refuse to give up their faith in the face of intense pressure to do so.

A celebrated recent case is that of Meriam Ibrahim, aged 27. She is a Sudanese Christian who was sentenced to death for allegedly renouncing Islam. She always maintained that she had never been a Muslim but a Christian. In an interview with Fox News of the USA she said, 'I was given three days to renounce my faith. The situation was difficult, but I was sure that God would stand by my side. It is my right to follow the religion of my choice.'

Ms Ibrahim was pregnant at the time of her arrest and later gave birth to her child, a baby daughter, Maya, in prison while shackled in chains. She was released after an international outcry. She described her faith as 'the only weapon I had in these confrontations with the imams and Muslim scholars' who were repeatedly sent to her to persuade her to convert to Islam.

She is well aware that her case is not an isolated one: 'There are many Meriams in Sudan and throughout the world. I'm not the only one suffering from this problem.'

Finally she says a great truth that we can all take to heart especially if we have been tempted to give up believing: 'If you don't have faith, you are not alive.'[2]

Meriam is right when she says her case is widespread. Sadly such persecution of Christians is now a worldwide matter and is spreading rapidly. We are supporters of the charity Release International, who offer support to persecuted Christians. The current edition of their quarterly publication, *Release*, gives details of suffering Christians in many countries, such as China, Egypt, India, Kenya, Nigeria, North Korea, Eritrea, Iraq, Iran, Sudan, Pakistan, Vietnam, Indonesia, Laos, Cuba, Mexico, Libya, Azerbaijan and Nepal. All the material is well documented. The magazine and Release International's other source materials are full of sobering but also inspiring stories of courage in the face of intense suffering from Christians who refuse to give up their faith. You might like to consider supporting them, or a similar charity, as well. We give Release International's contact details in the Resources section, together with those of similar organizations. Quite apart from the intrinsic good offering support like this would do (and there are many ways to help our persecuted brothers and sisters), it would also help us to keep to our own faith more strongly.

## *Meditation: Hebrews 11*

The greatest chapter on faith in the Bible is Hebrews 11. Please read it through. You will, we hope, find that doing this leads you into meditations enough of your own, but we will add one or two further thoughts for you to consider:

1 Note verse 3, which holds that the creation of the entire universe was an act of faith. If we are to be in tune with ourselves as creatures, the world in which we are placed and the God who created both us and it, then we need to be people of faith. Faith is vital, not the consumer option of current culture.

2 So vital in fact that 'without faith it is impossible to please God' (v. 6). In order to approach him we must believe that he exists. He is the rewarder of such faith. Our basis of communication with him is our faith. So it is well worth strenuously defending if we feel it slipping in any way.

3 Think through all the long list of the heroes of faith that forms the bulk of the chapter. What they have in common is that they all took risks on the basis of their faith in God. And from these risks came actions that brought about breakthroughs for both them and the people of God. What actions have we taken on the basis of our faith? What breakthroughs have come about for us in consequence? Are there encouragements to recall from our past faith that can uplift us now? What are the challenges to our faith now? How can we take new action to break through into new territories of faith?

Read the list of sufferings that ends Hebrews 11. They sound remarkably similar to articles to be found in *Release* magazine (see above). Consider doing more to support those Christians who are now suffering for their faith as did the heroes of old – 'the world was not worthy of them' (v. 38). You might like to turn to the next page of your Bible to find further urging to do this. Hebrews 13.3 says 'remember those in prison as if you were together with them in prison, and those who are ill-treated as if you yourselves were suffering'.

4 Finally, think about the life to come beyond this one. The heroes of faith were 'longing for a better country – a heavenly one'

(Hebrews 11.16). Their faith was inspired by belief in a life after this one, for which all their sufferings were worthwhile. How much can you envisage such a heavenly country? How invested in it are you?

## *Stressbuster: memorizing Scripture*

Take time to memorize a Scripture verse or passage. What we memorize goes deeper into our consciousness than when we simply read it, and it remains available to us when we can't read it.

> Lisa would meditate on the verse 'Peace I leave with you; my peace I give you' (John 14.27) at night when she was unable to sleep and worrying away at an insoluble problem. Repeating it to herself and allowing it to sink deep into her mind brought rest and eventually sleep.

We can also recall verses when we are on a commuter train or in the midst of a stressful day at work. To take scriptural truth deeper into ourselves in this way is de-stressing in itself.

Many Christians around the world with limited Bible resources have to commit Scripture to memory, and for those persecuted for their faith such a store of Bible verses is invaluable.

We learnt many verses as teenagers as part of the Navigators Bible learning scheme, as did one of our current colleagues. We have fun trying to recite these passages many years later, but we all three appreciate what a strong and underpinning effect knowing these passages has had down the years, and how they have come to our aid in difficult times. Some passages you might want to memorize are Psalm 23, Romans 8, Philippians 2.1–11 and 4.16. You may have a particular verse that speaks deeply to you that you can learn.

*Part 3*

# FAMILY LIFE

# 6

# *How can I manage my family life as a Christian?*

———•◦•———

## *Problem*

We don't suppose it's ever easy to be family, or ever has been, whether among Christian people or otherwise. In modern times, while we in the West don't have to avoid absolute poverty or a disease-ridden life, other concerns have surfaced about the pressures on family life. There is good evidence that the family is under extra pressure in modern times, a concern that even led a British government in the 1990s to open a special department about family life.

There is a higher divorce rate – 13 divorces an hour in England and Wales in 2012.[1] Many more people are bringing up children on their own, and children are not living as much with their natural parents – the number of children living within a step-family in Britain has risen by over 300,000 over the past 12 years and now stands at 900,000.[2] Many more people are living alone when they would rather not. All these factors have combined to give rise to general concern about patterns of family life in the country. Family life itself can be stressful, with complex relationships between different members of the extended family. Such stress can affect our faith and our church involvement, as is apparent from Mary's story:

Mary's stress was brought on by family circumstances when she was in her fifties. She had been made redundant a year prior to her father's death and had started to do a lot of voluntary work. She was churchwarden in her local church.

After Mary's father died her mother developed dementia and she had to work with her younger sister in making serious decisions about her mother's future. They had never had that sort of contact before.

Her sister had very strong ideas and liked to be in control of everything. Although she had always been like that, her father had always kept the peace. Mary had never liked conflict and now she felt she had to agree with her sister in order to avoid conflict in the family. Her sister wanted to decide everything herself and did not like it when Mary suggested they share out the jobs. She behaved as though Mary was out of order and made Mary feel inferior and incapable. Mary became very stressed about all that was going on and had to cut down on her voluntary work and resigned as church-warden. This made her feel very guilty and even more stressed.

Her faith in God did not waver and was a source of strength to her, as was her husband. Her advice to anyone suffering with stress is to get help as soon as possible.

It's a huge subject and in this short chapter we can only touch on particular issues of stress for Christians, and then only superficially.

## Marriage

Christians are not immune to marital stress. Elizabeth and I have been involved in many cases of counselling and mediation between Christian husbands and wives who are desperate about their marriage. There have been various outcomes – one happy one is worth mentioning. We spent an evening talking and praying with one couple about their marriage. When it was over they seemed to be feeling a lot better than when we started. We asked how things would go on from here and the husband said, 'Well, I drove here tonight with a suitcase packed and unless it was all right, I was leaving tonight. Now I feel I can go back home.' They went on to stay together and have more children and become a really solid family as part of our congregation.

There isn't always a happy outcome. Christians do get divorced and it can be an extra strain in a Christian context. Being a divorcee can bring stigma in a local church. It can affect people's office holding or sense of being welcome any more in their church, whereas when they were married all was well. A little example:

Jenny had been a strong member of her large church for a lot of years and deeply involved in the young people's work. There was a lot of gratitude to her from the parents of the young people for what she was doing with them. When her husband left her, in addition to that anguish, she felt the same body of parents did not trust her any more with their teenagers and she was subsequently asked to step down from that ministry in her church.

A further example of church difficulty over divorce would be the case of Jane and Richard, who were in one of our churches. Their marriage had been under strain and they decided to separate amicably, which they did. They both continued to attend our church but after a short time, Richard, against his wishes, left because he couldn't face the sense of stigma there was around now that he was separated from Jane. We tried hard to get him to stay and to get across the message in the church that we all ought to be bigger than that, but unfortunately he still felt he had to leave.

Another problem we've known with marriage is the opposite, where people have affairs and still expect to continue having prominent ministry in the church. In a neighbouring church two of its leading members, both of whom led services and preached, conducted an extramarital affair with each other. They were amazed and furious when the minister told them they could not continue to fulfil this ministry while conducting the affair. They both left the church, very angry and uncomprehending of what they might have done wrong.

The stress of a marriage in difficulties may be compounded because either or both partners are Christian leaders. Clergy marriages often buckle under the strain of the ministry. Balancing family life and church life is exceptionally difficult for church leaders. And the knowledge that a separation or divorce would be scandalous to the church and may cost one's job and home amounts to even more added pressure.

So these are just some of the ways the already very difficult issue of divorce or separation or extramarital affairs can be made even more complicated in a Christian context.

## Living together

Many more couples live together now, either for a period of time before marrying or with no view to marrying. Cohabitation has increased by 900 per cent in the last 50 years.[3] This too can bring stresses in a church context. One of the churches where we served felt that it should not offer baptism to the children of cohabiting couples. It's the only time that I, Andrew, have voted one way and the entirety of my church council voted another way. I felt we should not prohibit such baptisms. I agreed to go ahead with the policy providing a PCC member would come with me on the baptism visit just to sense the distaste this policy would bring about on the ground. Ironically, as is often the way in the kingdom of God, at the first visit the couple, while initially angry, did think about things, decided to get married as well as have their child baptized, and the woman in the partnership went on to be converted to Christ, confirmed into the Church of England and is a committed Christian to this day. So you never know. We sense this is something of a generational issue as well, with older-generation Christians disapproving of living together and younger people, on the whole, being much more laissez-faire about it. This can bring its stresses within the wider family, where, shall we say, the parent generation have grown children who live together rather than marry.

## Children

Of course it's always been hugely demanding to bring up children. Many more are brought up now in single-parent households, which can be very difficult in church life as well as in other ways. The issues around having no one with whom to share the burden, of having perhaps less money than other families, of getting babysitters and getting out to things, can affect someone's place in a church, and again there can be a sense of stigma on becoming a divorcee. We think of Carol, a member of one of our churches, who had been a good wife and mother but whose husband deserted her for another woman. She suddenly found she couldn't join in as she used to do and didn't feel she could attend church regularly because of the shame she felt. She also hadn't the time to get to church any more as she had to go back to work full time and was very tight for cash.

Even without the issue of single parenthood, trying to bring up children within the Christian faith can have extra, stressful factors. It takes love and care and tact as children grow older about how much to enforce a strong, Christian pattern of life on them. Whether to make them come to church when they don't want to is a delicate matter. There are so many competing activities, especially on a Sunday morning, that it often leaves parents with choices between valuable things like sporting events or seeing the wider family, and coming to church as a family. It's a very difficult one to win. Children can feel choked off and different from their peers if they're not joining in sporting and other activities on Sunday mornings but are being made to come to church. At the same time, Christian parents will want them to have a good grounding in the faith if for no other reason than having a Christian ethic as they face all the complex issues of sex, drugs, social media and internet use that children face at an earlier age and more intensely than ever. This conflict has been a really serious issue for most of the young families in our churches for the last 15 to 20 years. A tiny but illustrative example would be a family who apologized to us that their daughter would not be coming to a family service because she was going to a fellow classmate's birthday party. The school their daughter went to seemed to have a convention that the whole class was invited to every kid's party, which came to about 30 parties a year. Still, they felt that they had to prioritize this over church. It made us sad to see.

Finally, time pressure is very large in family life as in all else in modern society. Our newspaper of yesterday had on its front page an article entitled 'Children dropped off at school for ten-hour days'. It reported on a survey of 1,332 teachers by the Association of Teachers and Lecturers, half of whom stated that they 'had noticed within the past five years that children were spending less time with their parents and other close family'.[4] To blame, they felt, were divorce, long working hours, too much TV and games consoles. In our lifetime in the ministry we have seen young family involvement in our churches throttled by time pressure.

## Singlehood

We once did a quick survey of the largest church where Andrew was vicar, with a membership of several hundred people, and were surprised to discover that a third of all the adults on the church's membership list were single. At that time there was virtually nothing specifically for single people in our church's pattern of living – indeed the whole emphasis tended to be on family. A group was started called SWORD (single, widowed or divorced). It had a totally different feel to it from anything else in the church, with its own social life over the weekends when single people often feel lonely. Nearly everybody in it was not single by choice but from bereavement or separation or never having met anyone to marry. The level of mutual help and support the group created was remarkable. We had noticed that a lot of our single people avoided things like Mothering Sunday or our Christmas services, and we were able to run alternative things. It surprised us, the depth of emotional need that group found itself meeting. It helped us become aware that singlehood can, for the most part, be very stressful in itself for Christian people.

### Same-sex issues

Finally, we hardly feel we need say in the current climate how difficult the issue of same-sex relationships is in the Church. The issue of same-sex marriage has recently been hotly debated in the UK, with some sense that the Church is out of tune with the rest of society. We suspect that there have been many Christians of same-sex orientation who have had to keep it a complete secret to themselves or face extreme stigma in their churches. Mercifully this is now changing all the time but remains a very difficult issue all across many churches.

## *Opportunity*

'Every crisis is an opportunity.' This is our mantra for this book and here, with family issues, we think it no less. So let's look at what opportunities family stress can afford us.

First, and naturally, *it's an opportunity for us to look at our present situation in our family*, whatever it is, and do what we can to improve our family relationships. We may like to look in turn at our relationships with:

- our spouse or partner
- any children we have
- our parents
- any siblings we have
- our wider family – grandparents, aunts, uncles, nephews, nieces.

In each case it would be good to take a little time to dwell on the relationship concerned and think how things stand. It might be our chance to deepen our ties of family love and also to look at our overall priorities. Are we giving enough time and focused attention to our family life? This might bring a peace and reconciliation that we've never known before.

We might like to write a paragraph in our journal on each family relationship we have, noting what we find good there and what we value, but also what areas of pain there are. We might like to think over if there is any change needed on our part to make things better. We could also think of what changes in attitude we would like other family members to make towards us. It can be helpful to imagine what we would like to say to someone in our family if things are lying between us. It may need an external act – a prayer, a letter or something else. We may need help with it and might turn to our minister, a counsellor, our spiritual accompanier or some trusted friend.

There are excellent resources for married people to work on their marriage relationships. There are good parenting courses. There are good resources for those who lead a single life, either voluntarily or for want of having met a partner. There are agencies that specialize in helping with second marriages and the care of stepchildren. We give a selection of all these in the Resources section at the end of the book.

Second, *we could decide to become someone who prays systematically for family life* in this country. We can always pray. We can recall that 'The prayer of a righteous person is powerful and effective' (James 5.16). There are agencies whose purpose is to defend Christian values about family life. Perhaps the best known is Care for the Family, though there are others. They are all glad of prayer support and produce excellent materials to help people pray for their work. Of course, they do a lot more than this and we might be in a position to support them in more than prayer, by helping financially or going to their events or even holding such events ourselves. If we can help like this in any way we will be doing something to redress the balance towards good, stable Christian standards in family life.

Third, *we might be able to offer our time and concern into the family ministry of our local church*. Most churches do a great deal of work to help the family. There are usually baptisms, weddings and funerals – all of which offer opportunities for us to be involved with families at key times in their lives, assuming the minister is glad of such help, and most usually are. There are family services happening regularly is most churches and they all need a lot of input. There are mother-and-toddler groups, babysitting circles, old-people's work, listening services and a whole lot more, all of it family based and all of it chronically short-staffed. We could be doing invaluable work in these fields, with consequences for good far beyond what we can see. I recall meeting a young couple I had never seen before at my father's funeral. They had travelled a 100-mile round trip to be there. Dad had apparently at some stage done some marriage preparation for them – I did not even know he ever did this kind of work – and they had never forgotten its value to them. It had helped set them up for a stable lifelong marriage.

## *Inspiration*

For most of her life Anne had a difficult relationship with her mother, who seemed to be full of anger and rage, making Anne's and her sister's childhoods unhappy. As a Christian, Anne found her feelings towards her mother particularly difficult because even though she loved her and prayed, she could not forgive her. Even after her mother's death a tight band seemed to be woven round her heart.

Throughout her childhood the family had a close relationship with another family in East London. During the war, when Anne's family had moved to Somerset, this family came to visit in their car. The relationship continued after the war and Anne and her sister became very fond of the other family's daughter, Moira. Moira was seven years older than Anne. She was exciting to be with, always happy and noisy and had boyfriends, one of whom later became her husband. Moira had a son and about this time Anne herself married. Moira and family came to her wedding but gradually over the next few years Anne and Moira lost contact.

Thirty-eight years later, despite having searched the electoral roll and phoning everyone in that part of East London with a similar surname, and even driving up to London and searching for the old house, Anne thought she would never find her old friend Moira.

One day, after looking at the housing section of the local free newspaper, she dropped it on to the floor beside her. It was face down with back page uppermost, the sports page. Her attention was caught by the headline on it that read 'An act of stupidity'. For some inexplicable reason she felt drawn to read the article below. It was a report of a recent football match involving the local team, whose goalkeeper had been red-carded for charging an opposing player when he already had the ball. In the second paragraph the goalkeeper's name and age was given. His name was the name of Moira's son, and he would have been about the right age. Anne showed the article to her husband, and he felt sufficiently motivated to contact the club and leave contact details, just in case.

Sure enough, the goalie turned out to be Moira's son and a call came through from Moira – still loud and lively. She would love to renew contact. Could she come and visit? As luck would have it, this happened when Anne's sister was over making an extremely rare visit from Australia. Their father's 90th birthday was coming up and she had come over for that. So when Moira visited, Anne and her sister were both there. After the initial embraces and exclamations they sat down to talk. Anne did not really know what to expect but she recalls saying, 'Now, Moira, you must tell us everything about yourself. Don't leave anything out. We want to know.'

Moira's bright, outgoing expression changed at this. There was a pause and she said, 'I'm not sure you know where I fit in with you.' In an inspired moment Anne blurted out 'Moira, you're not our sister are you?'

She was not their long-lost childhood friend. She was their sister. Or, to be precise, their half-sister. She was the illegitimate daughter of their mother who, at that time, had been a single young woman working as a domestic servant in London, and had got herself pregnant by someone who never featured again in the story. She had had a difficult birth with Moira and needed to be in hospital for some weeks, with Moira in a cot beside the bed. On the other side of the cot, in the next bed, was a Mrs D. Mrs D's life hung in the balance. She had had three strokes and also contracted diphtheria. In her moments of lucidity, Mrs D delighted in baby Moira. She was a childless woman. Moira seemed to inspire her to rally. Over the weeks, she recovered, much to her doctors' surprise. It ended with Moira's mother giving Moira to Mrs D to adopt. She could not afford to keep the baby herself and had needed to put Moira up for adoption anyway. How much better to know Moira was going to a good home with someone whom she had got to know and would cherish her. Mrs D was overwhelmed and accepted, apparently saying, 'You must feel you can see her as much as you can. We must keep in touch.'

And so they had. This was the reason for the regular weekend visits from the D family, kept up even when Anne's family moved from London to Somerset. Mrs D's bad health earned them extra petrol rations and Mr D happened to be a driver with his own car, a rare thing then. Later Anne's family moved back to the London area and the visits were easier, but as the three girls grew up and got married, contact was lost.

Moira had had her suspicions about her origins off and on, but only had them confirmed after her mother's death, when she was left £100 in her will 'to my adopted daughter'. She had then traced her original birth certificate, giving her mother's maiden name and just a dash of the pen in the space for the father's name. She too had been searching for her sisters without success.

There were tears, many of them, and much catching up to do. And a sense of wonder at how God had brought them together in such a remarkable way. It turned out Moira too was a committed Christian.

Not long afterwards the three sisters were able to take a week away together in Scotland researching their mother, who came from Dunfermline. She had had a wonderful childhood with three brothers and another sister. Her parents started a business with a shop selling almost everything. They had a pony and trap and often went into the countryside for picnics. Sadly when Anne's mother was eleven both parents died within ten months of each other. The family split up, the boys going into the mines and the girls into domestic service. Leaving home young, having to make her own way as best she could in service, following the work from city to city and ending up in London, it was easy to see how she could fall for some young man who showed her affection.

As the story unfolded, Anne felt her tight band around her heart begin to unwind. She began to understand why her mother might have been as she was. She could see her lifelong heartbreak. She remembered her mother, at Moira's wedding, leaving her place halfway down the church to embrace Moira as she walked down the aisle. She had just been surprised at the time at this unusually forward show of emotion. Now it made sense.

Over time, Anne came to a place of complete reconciliation about her mother. The tight band went altogether. Her mother had been no saint, an angry embittered woman in many ways, and had done Anne lasting harm. But, for Anne, all that could now be left with God. And, wonderfully, she had gained a new sister. For her, like the father in the story of the Prodigal Son, all the loss was worth it because of the new life that had been gained.

And that wasn't the only new thing in Anne's life that came out of it. She started following the local football club!

## *Meditation: Luke 10.1–15, The parable of the Prodigal Son*

This parable is perhaps the best known of them all and is about family. We do an exercise based on the Prodigal Son when we lead sessions about family relationships. We ask people to get into threes: one of them takes the role of the father, one takes the role of the Prodigal Son and one takes the role of the elder brother. We have found it doesn't matter about gender here. Women seem as able to enter into this as men. The scene is the morning after the night before of the party when the Prodigal has returned. It is breakfast time. The three are sitting round the breakfast table talking about how they feel. That's it. Just the conversation. Then, after a set period, usually 45 minutes, roughly 15 minutes per person, we ask for feedback. We have found it just amazing what depth and variety comes out of this simple exercise. You might like to try it. You might be able to get into a threesome and do the exercise as three, but it's perfectly possible to do it on your own, taking each role in turn and thinking what each person has been through to arrive at that morning breakfast table – what they've had to suffer, what mistakes they've made, what sacrifices they've made, what they need to do to find a place of peace and reconciliation to the other two. We hope you might derive from this helpful insights into your own family relationships.

## *Stressbuster: imbibe some culture*

Often when we feel stressed out we lack the energy to engage with a good novel, film or play, rather preferring lighter, less demanding stuff. This is all right and a good way to relax, but over time there is a need to engage more deeply in order to keep being human and not simply functioning.

We despair of the number of times we have had a date in the diary to go and see a play or film and then cancelled because of overtiredness or overwork. We envy our friends who do get to concerts, plays and art galleries and return stimulated and nourished by the experience. We know we are missing out on something important. So put yourself in the way of some good culture. Visit an art gallery. Go to a concert. Watch a good film. Read a classic novel. Anything that touches your soul. It deepens us and brings in perspective amid all the hassle.

# 7

## *What am I to make of the sexual revolution?*

———•◆•———

### *Problem*

We don't suppose that the area of sexuality has ever been easy for most people, Christians or not, at any time, but it is arguable that Christians seeking to adhere to the Christian ideals on sexuality are under much more cultural pressure now than say two generations ago. Since that time the fundamental Christian ideal of sexual abstinence outside of marriage has become so alienated from mainstream sexual behaviour in our culture as to be almost laughable. It's broadly assumed that young people become sexually experienced in early or mid teens and the emphasis has been on education about good birth-control methods and other forms of hygiene and medical safety, rather than abstinence. The Kinsey Institute, which monitors social sexual activity, reported in 2002 that the average age for a male in the UK to become sexually active was 16.9 and for a female 17.4.[1] The ages are probably lower than that today. Despite being a nation that is one of the world's biggest users of contraceptives, a recent study has shown that the UK has the highest rate of teenage pregnancy in Western Europe.[2] On top of these broad statistics, any glance at the magazine rack in a newsagent or the romantic comedy section of a DVD store will show how society's attitude to sex outside of marriage is that it is a complete norm.

A final example might be the new phenomenon of sexting. According to Anne Mitchell, lead author of a recent study of Australian secondary students and sexual health, 'It's a social online world these kids live in. Sending these [explicit] messages is really a new form of courtship.'[3]

In the survey 84 per cent of those surveyed had sent explicit messages and over half had sent explicit photos of themselves. It is becoming an expected norm. Romance seems to have gone out of the window, and there are heartbreaking stories of young people who, after the breakup of a relationship, have found their explicit photographs posted on Facebook for all to see. Some handle their shame and humiliation by taking an overdose. Susie, a 15-year-old, was shocked to find that after she split with her boyfriend of a few months, he had sent an explicit photo of her to a male friend who had then uploaded it on to Facebook. In her embarrassment she felt the only way out was to end her life. Fortunately she recovered and had a supportive family, but others may not be so lucky.

This is a matter of pressure and stress for Christians. Christian young people wanting to adhere to the Christian ideal and trying to abstain from sex in anticipation of marriage will find themselves regarded as very odd. We think that hard as it's always been for healthy Christian young people wanting to keep their active sexual life for marriage, disciplining themselves nowadays must be harder than ever. Sexuality is pervasively explicit on the internet, in advertising and the mass media. It is so unquestionably the norm that one will become sexually experienced very early in puberty and have a number of sexual partners, that Christian young people wanting to keep to the Christian ideal must face severe pressure. Some Christians see the ideal as outdated, old fashioned and irrelevant to them, and see nothing amiss in living together before marriage.

We also think it must be a pressure for parents bringing up young people. They would like to see their children live to the Christian ideal in their adolescence and in their adulthood. It's never been easy to know how to promote this with one's children but in the same culture as we've just described, it is an additional pressure. Decisions have to be taken about overseeing children and young people when they want to start going out together. It's not easy to police whether or not they will be sexually active with each other. It can be the case that younger people these days will assume that they will sleep together and, for things like sleepovers or holidays, expect a double bed. Where Christian parents' children don't follow their parents' faith and assume that they will be able to sleep with a girlfriend or boyfriend under their parents' roof, that can be a source of stress.

We heard of married Christian parents who made a point of providing single beds in separate rooms for their son and his girlfriend when they came to stay, despite their protestations. They discovered how badly this had gone down when they next went to stay with the young couple and were themselves given separate beds and bedrooms!

The place of marriage as the unique and ideal place for sexual relationships is itself under pressure culturally. More and more people live together rather than get married. It's very rare now for any couple to marry who have not already set up home together. In the early 1970s in the UK fewer than 1 in 100 adults under 50 are estimated to have been cohabiting at any one time, compared with 1 in 6 currently.[4] The average age at which women first marry has gone up from 23 in 1978 to 30 in 2008.[5] It is so prevalent that people are marrying later in life that even the Church of England has produced a rite for marriage and the baptism of the couple's children to take place on the one occasion in church.

The place of marriage is still valued though, as we shall see further in the other sections in this chapter, but it is worth noting here the case of the celebrities Angelina Jolie and Brad Pitt, who married only after pressure from their children to do so. They went on to say how glad they were they had done so. Their relationship felt different and stronger in ways that surprised them.

There is also cultural pressure on marriage about the endings of marriage. The number of divorces has radically risen since the Divorce Reform Act of 1969. In 2012, 42 per cent of marriages ended in divorce compared to 22 per cent in 1970.[6]

This has had a huge effect on children. Only one-third of all the children in the UK now are resident with and being brought up by both their natural parents in the household. The churches have debated the issue of offering further marriage in church for those wanting to enter into a second marriage where an ex-partner is still alive. This has moved from being a rarity to being commonplace. In the Church of England diocese where we live and for which Andrew works, there has just recently been a directive from the bishop saying he doesn't want to know any more details of such marriages, which has been the practice before. He is happy now just to let local clergy proceed as in normal parish practice.

The recent move by the Prime Minister, David Cameron, to legalize homosexual marriage has brought the political mainstream into conflict with the churches. The present position of the Church of England is against homosexual marriage or the blessing of such a marriage if celebrated civilly in the church. Recent guidelines (February 2014) from the House of Bishops have been to advise clergy, if homosexual themselves, not to marry; for clergy not to offer formal blessings of same-sex marriages in churches; not to recognize same-sex marriage as marriage. There is evidence that the mainstream culture regard this stance as reactionary, and that younger Christian people feel the same. It can be extremely stressful for someone of homosexual orientation to be in a church. The sad case of the young girl who took her own life because she did not think her Christian parents nor her church would handle her newly discovered same-sex orientation is an extreme example.[7]

Finally, internet pornography has become a matter of real pressure for everyone. We think that Christian people are not exempt from this. We heard it said informally that three-quarters of all that is on the worldwide web is pornography. It's readily available at the click of a switch. We ourselves are coming across more and more ministers and other church leaders who find internet porn a lure and the growth of various Christian web organizations offering buddying arrangements and other forms of safeguarding seem also to indicate this.

## *Opportunity*

Not all is doom and gloom, even against this background of sexual licence all across society nowadays. There are some glowing exceptions.

There was the young man Cameron Stout who won the *Big Brother* TV show in 2003. He was a committed Christian. His choice as the one possession he was allowed to take into the house was his Bible. In the discussions in the house with other housemates he made no secret that he was a virgin and was planning to stay that way until he married his fiancée. This seems to have won the approval of the voters over other more colourfully behaved housemates.

There has also been the movement coming from the USA where people wear a 'purity ring' to show that they intend to stay chaste until they are married, which has been quite popular in schools.

There is a growing initiative also in schools for married couples to go in to answer questions about married life from sixth-form pupils. Churches often facilitate this and report strong interest from pupils. Further, the pupils nearly all want to form lifelong marriages. There was a good piece of research done a few years ago that found that married couples had greater sexual satisfaction than those in cohabiting relationships or who had a lot of casual sex.[8]

All these things are there for our encouragement.

In any event, it is worth remembering that while sexual sin is sin and is serious, it is not the worst of sins. We tend to feel a disproportionate amount of shame where we sin sexually – the Christian man who has a habit of looking at pornography, the Christian woman who has reason now to regret a promiscuous youth – may both feel very deep shame and self-loathing out of proportion to the sin. Sexual sins are sins of the flesh – they still are sins – but sins of the spirit, like pride and jealousy and hate, are much more destructive. It may even be that our sexual weakness can teach us a true humility of spirit that saves us from the worst sin of pride. Some people think Paul's famous 'thorn in the flesh' affliction, described in 2 Corinthians 11, was perhaps about a hidden sexual struggle he had, though this can only be conjecture.

Finally, one good thing about the sexual revolution is that it has created many more resources for help than there were before.

- There are good places of refuge, counselling and support for single mothers, particularly young ones, who find themselves pregnant without wishing it.
- There are support agencies for those who struggle with an addiction to pornography.
- There is an abundance of guidance in all types of media for having a fulfilling, varied and exciting sexual relationship with one's partner.
- There are sex therapists, some of them Christian, whose work is to help people have a good sexual relationship.

- There are good dating agencies for those seeking a partner, some of which are specifically for Christians.
- For those who are homosexual, there is an increasing atmosphere of understanding and tolerance replacing homophobia, both in secular society and in the Church, though it has to be said it would not be easy in many churches to come out as overtly homosexual, and there are organizations and movements dedicated to the support of homosexual Christian people.

We give a selection of contacts for all these supporting agencies in the Resources section.

## *Inspiration*

Philip Lyman, 18, is a pupil at Wellington College, Berkshire, a co-educational private boarding school. He recently 'outed' as a virgin in an article he wrote for the school's magazine in which he says:

> I believe that sex is an incredibly strong symbol of love between two people. Think of it as glue. Once you have had sex with someone, you're connected to them emotionally and physically. If you tear open that bond the rip leaves open scars where the glue once was. That's why casual sex never works in the long term, it just doesn't.

The article in *The Times* in which he is quoted goes on to say:

> He is one of a growing number of young people who were putting off sex until they had met someone significant. The most up to date health figures suggest he may be right. In 2011, 27 per cent of males aged 15–24 had not had sex, compared to 22 per cent in 2002.

It also reports that drinking among that age group is down. Just 1 in 8 of those aged 11–15 had drunk alcohol in the previous week in 2011, down 25 per cent from 2001. In Philip's view, drink usually accompanies young people losing their virginities. He says 'I would say that 90 per cent of people are drunk when they lose their virginity. It doesn't make them happy and it upsets me to see it.' Philip writes very frankly about the cost of his decision.

It takes a lot of self-discipline. There have been times when I could have gone and had sex with someone. I have had to step back and say 'No, I am going to regret it.' There are some incredibly good-looking girls here.[9]

It is inspiring to learn of young people like Philip Lyman making decisions such as this and then having the courage to speak out in public. Let us hope he is right that he is not alone but part of increasing numbers of his generation dong the same. And may it give us heart as we pray about the rising generation's view of sexual matters.

## *Meditation: John 8.1–11*

In this passage Jesus achieves that elusive balance between keeping to clear standards about sexuality and yet not being judgemental.

The issue suddenly erupts before Jesus. He's getting on with his teaching in the temple when they burst in on him, so there is an element of surprise. It's all very distasteful – they have the woman in their hands and thrust her into the middle. She might well have been wholly or partly undressed, which may account for why Jesus bends down and looks on the ground and writes in the dust. The whole thing is anyway a put-up job. Her accusers are not really bothered about the issue of adultery. They want to find some cause against Jesus' ministry and so they 'kept on questioning him' (v. 7).

Jesus is on the horns of a dilemma – if he says that she should not be stoned he is condoning adultery, and if he says that she should be, it looks savage and cruel. There was the rule under the Jewish law that the chief witnesses against someone threw the first stones when there was a verdict of stoning to death, and there was also a rule that witnesses were heard with the eldest first to give gravity to their testimony. This is why we read that once Jesus has given the classic statement 'Let any one of you who is without sin be the first to throw a stone at her' (v. 7), the crowd disburse, beginning with the eldest. The truth of course is that none of us is without sexual sin and for all of us it is a very volatile and fluid area. Out of all the areas of sinfulness, it's the one that is the least predictable and can erupt in otherwise respectable people, seemingly in any way and at any time.

Once Jesus is left with the woman he is able to deal with her very clearly and gently but succinctly and without condoning her behaviour – no one else has condemned her and so neither will he. He does add 'Go now and leave your life of sin' (v. 11).

We might like to think about our own sexuality somewhat and think what Jesus would say to us if we were brought before him in our nakedness about it. We might like to hear him say to us that we are not condemned for our wayward sexuality.

In our dealings with others we may benefit from trying to think what is the best balance between keeping to Christian standards and yet not being judgemental.

## *Stressbuster: do some good for others*

Those nearest to us often suffer most when we get very stressed, and are often taken for granted and neglected as we are preoccupied with our own needs. This Stressbuster is to renew contact with a friend or member of the wider family and do something with them he or she would enjoy.

Andrew invited his brother over, having not seen him for several months. He went birdwatching (sorry – birding) with him, as it was his hobby, in a local wildlife sanctuary. It was a lovely and instructive time, one that Andrew will never forget.

In addition to doing good to someone we know it is lovely to do good in the wider world, and as well as its intrinsic value, it helps you de-stress by taking your thoughts outwards and helps put your concerns in perspective. We imagine many of you do this already, but it may be something that has become neglected. However pressed you are, do a little bit of good to someone else. Make a donation. Write a letter. Pray for the work of a charity near your heart. It breaks up the self-preoccupation stress brings with it.

*Part 4*

# CHURCH LIFE

# 8

## *How can I fit church into my pressured life?*

---·•·---

### *Problem*

A major part of the additional stresses Christians can bear that non-Christians don't is to do with church involvement. On the whole Christians go to church – it is an important place for us. Many of us will have been brought up to go to church – it's something we've done all our lives. Even if this is not the case and our Christian commitment has come at a later stage, going to church will be central to our faith journey. We set great store by it.

We imagine we're addressing Christians with two types of problem about the stress they feel through the time given to their church.

The first, which we look at in this chapter, concerns those who feel that because of all the other stresses they face in their life, they don't get to church nearly as much as they should. The second, which we look at in the next chapter, is about Christians who give too much time to church.

We begin here with those who worry about not getting to church as much as they used to.

### Regular attendance

Statistics show that people's overall *regularity in attending church has become less frequent*. Even though in some cases Christians might regard themselves as firm members of their church, the overall regularity with which they attend is decreasing. We did a survey in our own small benefice here during last year about the whole life of our worship. The average regularity with which responders to our questionnaire attended church was quarterly. All those responding would have regarded themselves as seriously belonging to our church and attending reasonably regularly. The pattern of weekly attendance from most of a church's committed membership seems to be a thing of the past. A minister friend of Andrew's said to him recently: 'I never know who I'm going to be looking at on any one particular Sunday.'

There are all kinds of good reasons for this.

- Working life no longer has regular hours – people are expected to work longer hours and often across weekends.
- Family life is more diverse – members of a family will often live further apart geographically than was traditional and weekend travel is necessary to keep in proper touch. Or we may be looking after a family member who is unable to attend church with us.
- Many other good, recreational activities now take place on Sundays. This is particularly true for young people's sporting and other activities. Christian parents are often torn between attending church or having their children in these activities that are good for them. There is also strong peer pressure among children and young people about them and parents don't want their children to be the odd ones out.

### Services

Another factor in it being more difficult to get to church are *the types of service*. We live in a society that has encouraged individual choice and in which we have come to expect to have what we want. People are more often going to those services that appeal to them. This is again particularly true of younger families, who will typically only aim to get to the monthly family service and not go to any others. But it can be equally true of other people who may opt only to go to, say, the 1662 Prayer Book service when it is happening in their church, and that also is not likely to be on a weekly basis nowadays.

### Age

Another factor is *age*. Many churches have ageing congregations. When someone becomes too infirm to attend or can only do so by being dependent on others to get there, it can be distressing. No matter if Holy Communion is taken to them in their homes or some equivalent care is put in place, they still miss being in the church building on a Sunday along with everyone else, often after a lifetime of being there every week. Irrationally they can feel a failure or a burden on others. It is another loss in life among many losses of independence at such a time. And death seems moved a stage closer. All this is seriously stressful.

So for reasons like this we imagine there will be those reading this book who find they are not getting to church as they used to and have bad feelings about it.

- These might be feelings of an underlying guilt that we are losing touch with God and our faith.
- There might be stress caused by disagreement within the family about how often to try and get to church. One parent might feel that it is important to go weekly or at least fortnightly and that the children may have to sacrifice some of their sport; the other parent may feel the opposite.
- Getting less regular at attending church often goes with feeling that we are too busy generally. As a minister I (Andrew) have lost count of the times I have heard 'Sunday morning is the only time we get' as an excuse for not coming to church. If this is true then those people are finding themselves caught in a lifestyle that is far too stressful overall. If you are down to only having a couple of hours a week on a Sunday morning as downtime then you are badly overstretched. It becomes important then to review our commitments and address our overall lifestyle.
- Concomitant with this is a sense of the loss of control of our own lives. We don't find people are attending less out of a deliberate decision to thin out their attendance. They just don't have the control to plan it in as they would wish. They have a feeling that they ought to get there but never seem to manage it, what with everything else. This lack of control over what people are actually doing and what they are not is in itself stressful. To have your life running you rather than you running it creates an underlying disorder that erodes contentment and creates stress.

## *Opportunity*

If we are not getting to church as much as we would like, now is an opportunity to address that. It would be good to take some time over this rather than try and think about it on the hoof. You might like to block in some time to sit down with your notebook or journal, a cup of coffee at your side and a pen in your hand.

Have a think about *how often you would like to get to church and why you go, then be realistic and write down how often you are actually going*. (There may need to be a reality test here. We might need to use a diary to check just when we did and did not get to church. In our work, Elizabeth and I usually find that people think they're going to church about twice or three times more often than they actually are.) Then think what feelings the gap between how often you go and how often you might wish to go leaves you with. You might like to make a prayer to God and try to sense what he would say in reply.

You could go on to answer the question of *what stops you going as often as you would like* – what other things stand between you and being at worship regularly enough. Again, write them down. Common answers would be:

- the children's sport
- the children's social life, parties and the like
- one's own recreational interest
- tiredness
- a sense of its being the only time in the week when we can relax or just be ourselves.

Your answers may of course include others. Once you've written them down, look at them and again note what feelings they evoke in you – and again perhaps make a prayer and see what you feel God is saying to you about them.

Finally, think about *any action you wish to take*, what this leads to and whether there is anything you might wish to change. It may be that this exercise has reconciled you to what you do now and you can feel less guilty about it – and if so, well and good. It may be that there are ways you could get to church more regularly by altering priorities, and that you and your family would be better for that.

## *Inspiration*

There was in one of our congregations a married mother of two young children, Sally. Sally had been on the fringes of the church congregation from girlhood. She had married in the church and had her children baptized there but she had not otherwise attended more than once or twice a year. She did start attending a midweek mother-and-toddler church discussion group that we brought into being. She appreciated it and gradually found she wanted to attend Sunday services more regularly but feared an adverse reaction from her husband, who had no interest in the church at all. She was also a busy person. She had a part-time nursing job and growing children who she wanted to participate in the normal activities for their age, many of which took place on a Sunday morning. She came to us for a conversation about it, explaining that her outlook was changing.

> I used to see it as – there was me in the centre and next to me was Sam [her husband] and then the children and then their grandparents, a bit further out, and then friends and the school and work and the church, all a bit further out still. And then things like good causes and life in the city and so on. And it was all all right. But now it's changing. I'm not sure what's happening but I don't feel easy with having me at the centre any more. It's not nearly as comfortable any more. I feel I have to change things but I'm scared of losing my family and what I have.

We talked on. We tried to assure Sally that God did not want her to lose her family or her career either but that, yes, he would rightly expect to be at the centre and not she herself – and that she may have to trust him and take some risks.

Sally started coming to church very regularly and went on to become a full participant in church life, especially in family things. Her husband did not prove to be at all antagonistic. He would come occasionally and would help with practical things. He was a good photographer and we still have a nice framed photo of the church that he once gave us as a gift. Her children came to all our children's activities and did much else besides. She continued her nursing career. She also gained a strong personal faith.

We believe that Sally stands as an example of the good that comes from prioritizing the things of God at risk to other important things. We make no bones about it – we think that getting to church regularly is worth fighting for in the teeth of many other understandable pressures.

## *Meditation*

In our meditation section in this chapter we just take the single verse from the Psalms, 'I rejoiced with those who said to me, "Let us go to the house of the Lord"' (Psalm 122.1).

We suggest you say this verse to yourself several times over. Note what sort of imagery comes to you as you do so. It might be biblical imagery of worshippers in the days of David, who wrote this psalm, making their way to worship in Jerusalem, or might be contemporary imagery to do with your own attendance at your church or at a conference or some such. It might be neither of these, but do note what images come to you.

Second, and again you may like to have used the verse several times over to yourself, swirling it round in your head as you might swirl brandy in a glass. Note your feelings. What feelings does this verse stir in you? Are they positive? Note those that are positive. Can you share in the psalmist's rejoicing at the thought of going to the house of the Lord to worship? We hope there will be more than one positive feeling – feelings perhaps of awe, reverence at drawing near to God; of fellowship, commonality, sharing in the company of fellow worshippers; of familiarity and love of our surroundings as we go again to worship; positive feelings of our history and tradition and a long-standing practice.

It is equally important to note any negative feelings. The verse may invoke feelings of regret that we don't feel this any more, we can't go to church any more or that we have let things slip; feelings of wistfulness and nostalgia and loss; feelings that maybe we have been on the wrong end of something divisive and difficult in our church life and that this verse evokes it in a negative light – we are far from rejoicing about going to the house of the Lord.

When we have noted these feelings, it is good, as we say in the Introduction to this book, to keep a journal and write these things down, and also to discuss them with your spiritual accompanier. What does thinking about this verse from Psalm 122 make you want to do, if anything? Make a resolution.

## *Stressbuster: reflection*

For the Stressbuster in this chapter we recommend a practice we ourselves have found invaluable and that we use with our counselling clients all the time. It is simple and is drawn from Ignatian spirituality. It goes like this: at the end of every day, take a moment to reflect on the best thing that has happened to you that day. Dwell on it until you have exhausted its goodness. Don't be tempted to move off it. Stay with it, swilling it round in your mind, again like brandy in a glass. We also use the idea of sucking a sweet. To get the best out of the sweet you leave it on your tongue, savouring the taste, resisting the temptation to crunch it up too quickly. You will be surprised at the power of this simple exercise. It is especially useful done last thing at night if you struggle to get to sleep. Once it's done you can then move on to another good thing that has come back to mind by recalling the first good thing – and then a third good thing and so on. Often this can quite change your view of the day from overall negative to positive.

# 9

## *How can I stop my church stressing me out?*

### *Problem*

The other type of problem that we imagine affects people about time given to the church is the opposite of the one in the last chapter. Instead of feeling that they are not giving enough time to church, there are other Christians who devote almost too much time to it.

### Too much

It is difficult to be a conscientious church member and not regularly be approached to take on further roles in the church on top of attending Sunday by Sunday. All denominations have loads of councils and committees and groups in order to function.

- There are parish church councils to staff.
- There are elders, churchwardens, lay ministers needed.
- There is the young people's work that needs adults to run it.
- There is church music, a choir or band to join in.
- There is the old people's work.
- There are community roles like becoming a school governor.
- There is the ecumenical work in any locality where churches work side by side on projects.
- There may well be interfaith work on top.
- In many churches, in addition to Sunday worship there is also a range of midweek devotional groups.

We may, as conscientious Christians, have been brought up to regard attending midweek Bible study as as strong an imperative as attending church on a Sunday morning. If we attend regularly we will probably soon be asked to lead one, and that is a further demand on time. If you take up any roles on top of just being a church member, not only is there the time involved in going to the meetings to do with that activity, there is often preparation for it: Sunday school lessons need preparing; church council meetings involve a lot of paper-work that has to be read in advance. Church life simply gobbles time up, and those willing will soon find themselves holding three, four or five significant roles in the church in addition to going along to worship.

Pat had worked in her local church Sunday school for 18 years, which often put a lot of stress on her own family. She would have to be out of the house promptly on Sunday mornings, which wasn't easy with children of her own, and would also give extra time, such as taking young people on weekends away or to fun activities or holiday camps.

She found running the Sunday school very stressful after about 15 years, and gave up entirely three years later. She puts her stress down to changes, first, in the attitude and culture both at church and, second, among the parents of the children. At church she found that decisions were being taken by the leadership about the Sunday school without any reference to or consultation with her. At the same time she noticed that parents were 'always taking' and didn't ever acknowledge the effort put in to run the groups each week, and often ignored her. She felt that this was a reflection of the prevailing culture where people are keen to take what is on offer but not to commit to offering help themselves.

Pat remained a regular member of her local church and said that she never confused her feelings about church with her faith in God. However, she says that now she is unlikely to take on any serious work in the church.

In our experience in leading local churches for nearly 40 years, you could divide the congregation into those who don't come often enough and seem unable to maintain a regular life of worship, and those who do come regularly but get saddled with far too much being expected of them. These tend to be the conscientious types who have a high sense of duty, worrying that if they don't take on jobs they'll be disappointing God and the minister. They fear that the church won't function any more if they are not willing horses. Some of this is a generational problem. Church congregations, taken overall, are ageing and shrinking. Overactive church members are often getting on in years and under the stress of thinking they'd really like to stop and retire now, but who's going to take their place? They are driven by anxiety that if they stop they will see their beloved church fold up altogether.

## *Opportunity*

As in the foregoing chapter about those who are finding that they are not getting to church as they wish, there is, for those who are feeling overcommitted at their churches, the opportunity to take stock.

It would be good, if you feel this way, to settle down with your journal or some other way of noting things down on paper, and *write down all your actual commitments* in the life of your local church. Once it is written, take a look at it and then note down the feelings and reactions the list provokes. Does it seem a reasonable amount of work for you? It's probably worth noting as well other commitments away from church – to workplace, family and so on. In the light of all this we might well ask ourselves whether we need to shed some of these commitments. It might be that we bear them well, enjoy all we do and want to keep going. People's capacities differ and, in our experience, there are those at the heart of local church life who take on very large amounts of work but find it overall right and fulfilling for them. Equally, it might be right that we lay down some tasks to leave ourselves a more reasonable burden of responsibility in the local church.

Another opportunity thrown up by this consideration of our local church life is *to take stock of all that the church means to us*. We might like to write something down about why we go to church at all, and also why we go to our particular church. What is our history with it? What is our debt to our church? In what ways has it helped us?

When I, Andrew, tried out this exercise after a lifetime of professional service to the Church of England, and feeling deeply weary of it all, I was overwhelmed by the benefits I felt I had received from the Church. It lightened my outlook considerably, and so it may do for yourself as you do this exercise. There will be many people to whom we are indebted, who have inspired us, who have given us sacrificial service in the way that we are now perhaps being asked to give it to others.

We may want to assess if *it's time for a change of the type of local church* we belong to. One of the glories of the Church is the huge variety of ways of worship and of Christian traditions that there are. We know of someone who had a lifetime in the Conservative Evangelical tradition of the Church of England and had found that nourishing, but now, in middle life, that seemed to have dried up on this person, who made a very beneficial change to the Anglo-Catholic tradition with its more ritualistic, meditative spirituality. Something akin to this may be right for us.

A final consideration of our local church is an opportunity to remember just what the church is – *a lifeboat not a luxury liner*. We go there because we are in the business of seeking the salvation of our own souls and that of others. It's not a be-all and end-all – it's a way of making a voyage away from our sins and towards salvation in heaven. We can therefore expect hardships and danger and difficulties on the way. It's worth remembering that.

## *Inspiration*

### Three cross bearers

For our inspiration in this chapter we think of three different people who were the cross-bearers in three of our parishes. Their job was to carry the ornamental cross at the head of the ceremonial liturgical procession of the choir and ministers at the start of our acts of worship. Two were men and one a woman. All three had a disability of some kind. Let's call them Martin, Richard and Lindy.

Martin was physically disabled and also had learning difficulties. He was not able to do too much in terms of office holding in the village church where he had grown up and was a deeply committed member. But he was able to carry the processional cross and did it for many years. He treasured his being in the role and so did the congregation. By the time I, Andrew, became the incumbent it was becoming more and more of a struggle for him to do it any more. He was no longer young and a condition of his back meant he had to stoop, which made it difficult. He often half-stumbled. Nonetheless, he persevered. There were many services where we all held our breath hoping he would not fall. And it seemed to take for ever for him to get to the front of the church and be able to put the cross down. When he did get there we all breathed a silent sigh of relief. Not too long after my arrival Martin needed to enter residential care, where he was very content for a few years, lovingly visited daily by his sister, also a member of the congregation. And so his cross-bearing had to stop. I had the privilege of taking his funeral a year or two later.

I mention him because he seems to me a symbol of our service to God in church. We all wondered if he would make it week by week. He was so frail. Indeed he looked not unlike the figure of Christ carrying his cross in a Passion Play, stooped and stumbling. But he kept on. He regarded it as a privilege. And he kept on right to the end, winning all our hearts. When I lack inspiration or feel tired in my church work, I often think of Martin and feel I'll stumble on until I really can't do it any more.

Richard was the physical opposite of Martin, tall and strong though also learning disabled. I recently returned for the first time in over 20 years to the church he belongs to and where I was once the incumbent. It was a big anniversary for the church and I met Richard over tea and cakes before the anniversary service began. We caught up. Little had changed for him. He still lived alone in the small sheltered flat I recalled. He still had the same job. He still went on walks with the Christian Walkers' Fellowship as his main recreation at weekends and for his holidays. Altogether Richard looked the same, as tall, strong and clear-eyed as ever. I recalled our Fund Raising Committee meetings at his small flat, when he had been the perfect host. I'd forgotten, just then, that he was the cross-bearer for the church but once we'd settled for the service and he came down the aisle, robed and boldly carrying the cross, it came back to me. He too in his way, like Martin, symbolized something important about Christian belonging. The church had given Richard home and significance that he could not have easily had elsewhere. He had also served the church staunchly and steadily. The Book of Common Prayer talks about God 'whose service is perfect freedom'. Richard had had a durable, fulfilling life of service when he might have been a very lonely person on the edge of society. We too, if we will serve willingly, will find its rewards are deeper than anything we can otherwise gain.

I took Lindy's funeral recently. She was 66 years old. Lindy had not been expected to live beyond childhood. When she was 50 there was a huge party for her because she had not been expected to live that long. She was born with a genetic condition that meant she lived in a body with a height of 3 feet 6 inches. She spent her life fighting for survival. But she did much more than survive. She was for years at the very hub of village and church life. She was a parish councillor, a church councillor and secretary to the Village Hall Committee. Nothing went on in the village without her having a hand in it. She organized the Queen's Jubilee celebrations in 2012. She did the Summer Fair most years. In recognition of her community service she received, not long before she died, the British Empire Medal, leaving her hospital bed to go to the ceremony. In church, she had been in the choir since she was a girl – and she also carried the ceremonial cross, tiny as she was, not always but sometimes. She was absolutely indomitable. She too is an inspiration to me. She shows just what the human spirit is capable of. The church was packed for the funeral, all touched by her. A curious thing was that a beautiful butterfly fluttered around all over the church during the service. It went in and out of the rays of the sun that came in through the windows. At the wake afterwards, many remarked on it. It seemed a symbol – both of her indomitable yet vulnerable self and of the resurrection. Whenever I feel like giving up in my service to God, I think of Lindy and decide I can keep going.

## *Meditation*

Two short parables that counterbalance each other:

### The parable of the Unworthy Servants (Luke 17.7–10)

This little-known parable from the teachings of Jesus is not often dwelt on. It gives us a somewhat unfashionable but important message. We often think of our belonging to church as if we are doing God a favour by going and by doing what we do there. In fact we should rightly count ourselves lucky to be allowed into the church at all and thankful that the church even exists for sinners like us. This parable reminds us that when we've done all our faithful work, it's only what God might rightly expect from us and what we might rightly expect to do for him.

### The parable of the Watchful Servants (Luke 12.35–38)

It is, though, worth counterbalancing it with this similar passage where Jesus speaks of faithful servants who are found by God to have kept good watch for their master all night long and how the master himself would sit them at table, put an apron on himself and serve them. It's right from this to infer that God delights in our service, will reward us for it in good time and is pleased with us for offering him our sacrifice in serving his people in our local church.

## *Stressbuster: creativity*

A couple of years ago we ran two seminars on stress for an Anglican diocesan study day. There were 600 delegates and our seminars were both full. We listened to many stories of overcommitment and stress from keen church members. When we suggested people might rediscover their creative side as a way of combating stress, one young woman spoke up to say, 'I used to do lots of sewing and really enjoyed it but since I have become churchwarden I don't seem to have the time. My machine just sits there in the back of the room.'

We asked her how long it had been since she had used it. She thought for a moment and then said, 'Five years!' It came as a shock to her that it had been so long. Unfortunately when we take on a lot at church on top of our ordinary lives, that is how it can be.

Expressing our creative side is an excellent Stressbuster and uses the right half of our brain. Think what creative things you enjoy – writing, drawing, painting, sculpture, cooking, gardening, dancing, singing, acting. Anything creative. The self-expression this gives is most valuable. Decide to get back to doing something regularly. You might like to make some notes in your journal about this.

# 10

## *How do I cope with church politics?*

---◆•◆•◆---

### *Problem*

The subject of this chapter follows on from that of the previous one and is about further stress factors that very frequently come into play for Christians within their church life if they are seriously committed to it. In addition to the sheer stress that time pressure alone can bring, which we looked at in the last chapter, usually in church life there is a whole lot more stress to do with the politics of the place.

Churches are by no means immune from internal politics. Everywhere has them. If you have an organization, you have politics. In churches they can frequently be extremely stressful. The pressures of being a minister or in senior lay leadership of a local church are very intense. In our view, after a lifetime of involvement, church politics can be unbelievably stressful. They are often bitterly fought out and absorb, often wastefully, huge amounts of time and worry.

Here are a couple of examples we have witnessed from close at hand recently, neither of them in our denomination.

First, two churches of the same denomination, less than a mile apart, each with falling congregations, were considering amalgamation. One (very valuable) site would be sold and the money used to develop the other to create first-class church and community facilities. Two years' worth of consultation work was done with the congregations, denominational leaders and the local community. Finally the full two-thirds majorities were secured at the relevant church meetings needed to authorize the plans. Then, and only then, a small minority of opponents within one church got active. They managed to scupper the whole thing using arcane regulations within the denomination that their lawyers dredged up from somewhere. One minister resigned through ill health induced by stress, and that church is now leaderless. The scheme is now mothballed. Both churches continue to decline.

Second, a large, successful church took a risk by appointing a high-flying young minister instead of the usual fifty-something experienced sort. Unfortunately it went wrong and the young minister had to resign. He ended up with no marriage and no job. This was stressful enough all round. The leadership of that church then set about finding a replacement. After several more months' work they proposed the new candidate to the church meeting, which required a 75 per cent majority to approve. Opponents of the new man organized a number of people who were entitled to vote, but had not come to church for a long time, to attend the meeting and vote against. The meeting only secured a 68 per cent majority. So this church continues to drift. They need to start again from scratch and are haemorrhaging people fast.

We could multiply examples of this sort many times over. Imagine the stress levels involved. Imagine being a minister or conscientious lay leader in either of those situations. Imagine the hours you have put in. Imagine the energy you have expended. Imagine the hopes and excitements you have worked through. Imagine the fury you feel at the skulduggery of the few bad-minded people. It adds up to a lot of stress.

No wonder ministerial stress levels are seriously worrying denominational leaders. A new interdenominational counselling service for minsters has come into being to help with the problem.[1] Our diocese of Rochester has taken the step of offering clergy and their spouses sessions of stress counselling at its expense, no questions asked. The offer has been very widely taken up. That of course is just for ministers. Lay church leaders suffer the same stresses and have to cope with secular jobs as well, which can be equally stressful.

There are perhaps three reasons why the stresses of church leadership are worse than ordinary ones.

*First, the issues that are at stake in running a church are often more intensely debated and more hotly defended than those in commerce. I,*

Andrew, recall a time in one of my churches when we had a sustained period of profound disagreement in our church leadership, such that it nearly broke my mental health and wasn't doing a power of good to all of us involved, friend or foe. Ultimately formal, mediation procedures were needed. I recall, in a moment of truce, just asking my lay colleagues how they were getting on because they all had major jobs in commerce to do as well – I was the only one full-time in the church. They replied that their commercial life was just a job and they could take it or leave it but these issues in the church's life to them were life and death: indeed, they were even more – they were to do with eternal life. So there we were, fighting each other more bitterly than if we'd been in business.

*Second, progress in church life is simply getting more difficult.* In most churches attendance is declining and the church congregation as a whole is ageing. This brings with it knock-on stressful effects. There are fewer people to go around to run the church. Finding people for the major offices within the church without which it can't really run, such as treasurers, secretaries, churchwardens and elders, is ever harder. The money issues in church, which have never been easy, spiral upwards with rising costs. There are fewer people in the church to contribute towards meeting these costs, and the current period of economic austerity (2010–14) affects people's ability to give. Churches regularly have historic buildings to maintain that are expensive. They can be inefficient in terms of the use that's wanted from them and the procedures to modernize them very cumbersome. Congregation members are finding it harder to give time and commitment into the church, as we have described in Chapters 4 and 8. This leaves those who do undertake a commitment to keep the church on the road with a relentless timetable of meetings and seemingly insoluble issues, which can be seriously depressing.

*Third, the cultural drift away from Christianity is a factor in this.* We will discuss this in rather more detail in Chapter 14, but it has led to a thinning out of ministerial and lay leadership in the countryside, so that ministers often find themselves responsible for a number of communities and can't really belong to them all adequately. In the urban areas, multicultural and multifaith factors kick in more strongly and can lead to a dilution of the role of the church in communities.

Everything said so far is to do with the local church. For those whose Christian involvement takes them into the wider church at regional and national level, it can often be harder still. Much regional and national work is in any case done in addition to commitment to the local church on a voluntary basis. Even a cursory knowledge of the media coverage of church affairs at a national level will convey the high levels of stress there are there. This work can seem even more thankless than working at a local level, where at least we are in immediate touch with those we are trying to help and can sometimes at least see the rewards. At a national level this is much less apparent.

So make no mistake – the church can be a very tough place to be.

## *Opportunity*

It might seem, having given such a dire description of what church politics can be like, that they don't produce any opportunity at all except the opportunity to get out! But as with the other chapters in this part of the book, we would again ask you to do some stocktaking in order to gain a right perspective on what you are undergoing.

The church has always been full of agonizing issues. In the second epistle of Paul to the Corinthians we read of a Paul who is deeply wounded by a number of false accusations, political manoeuvres behind his back and a sense of betrayal by a church he had spent a long time with and deeply loved. In sustained passages, his raw anger and pain at this are very apparent. We set out some references for this in the Meditation section below.

For all this, Paul did not give up on the Corinthian church, nor did he stop his work as an Apostle. Indeed, the very goings on at Corinth cause him to list his sufferings for the church, and very impressive they are (see 2 Corinthians 11.21—12.10). It may well be right that, even though we are deeply embroiled in very painful church political issues, we are in the right place and our suffering, while agonizing, may well be the cross of Christ for us and a right form of suffering.

As touched on just now, we were, for some years, embroiled in a bitter battle in one of our churches, and more than once thought of resigning and leaving them to it. But somehow it never felt right. We felt called by God to go to that place, we still felt that the majority of church members supported us, and those who wanted rid of us were not representative of the broad membership even though they held a lot of political power. We felt we should stay there. It was extremely stressful. At that same time we had four teenage children to care for who were themselves, as teenagers tend to, in need of a great deal of our attention and, off and on, causing us grief enough of their own.

This kind of scenario may be God's calling for you right now. We won through to a place we would now feel was right for us to have fought for, and we had fruitful times thereafter. Again the same may be right for you. The kingdom of God comes in through 'many hardships' (Acts 14.22), and church leaders are regularly called to go through them for the good of that kingdom.

Equally it may be that you have been sucked into a vortex of church infighting that is wasteful of your time and everybody else's. Satan loves to get Christians fighting against each other and the more he can multiply contentious meetings without real decisions being made, the more he can bog churches down in senseless controversy, then the happier he is. And it might be right for you to walk away from all this.

You may find it helpful, again, to use the basic techniques of just writing out something about your present situation and then thinking about what you have written. You may like to show your writing and share your thoughts with somebody outside the situation who would give a considered view. This is where having a spiritual accompanier would be especially valuable. It may be that you need to tender your resignation or walk away from the particular political church scene that you are involved in at the moment.

Overall, writing after nearly 40 years of professional involvement in the church and a lifetime of being regular worshippers, we want to say that the difficulties and sufferings involved in being seriously committed to one's local church are well worth it. It's amazing how God seems to sustain an inner flame despite so many pressures, strains and discouragements.

## *Inspiration*

Sometimes amid all the hardship of church leadership we can become very downbeat and wonder if it's all worth it. As a counterbalance to this, here are some encouraging facts about the growth of the Church worldwide.

In his book *Witness Essentials*, Dan Meyer[2] lists some encouraging statistics about the growth of the Church around the world:

- In 1900 Korea had no Protestant church. Today there are over 7,000 churches in just the city of Seoul, South Korea.
- At the end of the nineteenth century the southern portion of Africa was only 3 per cent Christian. Today, 63 per cent of the population is Christian, while membership in the churches in Africa is increasing by 34,000 people per day.
- In India 14 million of the 140 million members of the 'untouchable' caste have become Christians.
- More people in the Islamic world have come to Christ in the last 25 years than in the entire history of Christian missions.
- In Islamic Indonesia the percentage of Christians is now so high (around 15 per cent) that the Muslim government will no longer print statistics.
- Across the planet, followers of Jesus are increasing by more than 80,000 per day.
- Some 510 new churches form every day.

## *Meditation*

Paul's two epistles to the Corinthians are very instructive to those feeling the pressures and strains of church life, especially of church leadership. Just a cursory flick through of the pages of them, particularly if your Bible has headings, shows the kind of issues Paul was wrestling with, and the stress the Corinthian church gave him. There were:

- divisions in the church (1 Corinthians 1.10–17 and 1 Corinthians 3.1–9);
- immorality in the church (1 Corinthians 5 and 1 Corinthians 6.12–20);

- church members taking each other to court (1 Corinthians 6.1–11);
- disputes about marriage (1 Corinthians 7);
- uncertainty about eating food sacrificed to idols (1 Corinthians 8);
- arguments about who has the authority in the church (1 Corinthians 9);
- issues about the Church's life of worship (1 Corinthians 11—14).

We imagine some of these issues sound very familiar to readers who are involved in the pressures of church life.

In 2 Corinthians we see even more of the pain and cost to Paul of church leadership. There are several passages in it that we have turned to in times of extreme stress in our calling to be church leaders: 2 Corinthians 4.7–17, 2 Corinthians 6.3–13 and the sustained passage over two chapters, 2 Corinthians 11 and 12, especially 2 Corinthians 12.7–10 – one of the most famous pieces of Paul's writing. These all show Paul's raw emotions as he is driven to distraction by the divisions and false accusations coming out of the Corinthian church. We especially treasure 2 Corinthians 6.9–10 as a description of life under pressure for the Christian church leader – 'known, yet regarded as unknown; dying, and yet we live on; beaten, and yet not killed; sorrowful, yet always rejoicing; poor, yet making many rich; having nothing, and yet possessing everything'.

So please, if you're feeling the pressures of church life at the moment, enjoy a trot through 1 and 2 Corinthians.

## *Stressbuster: play*

As a good antidote to the usually overintense and draining world of church politics, we suggest as the Stressbuster for this chapter rediscovering the child within us and playing. This can be as simple a thing as getting out a jigsaw and doing it, or playing a game of cards or a board game with someone. Of course, it can connect with other things we are suggesting, like exercise and playing sport or playing a musical instrument, but the key element is just to let one's hair down and have fun. You could do worse than just get a child's colouring book and fill it in, as we do alongside our grandchildren sometimes. It's surprising how relaxing and therapeutic even that can be.

So have a think. When was the last time you played a game of any kind, and how can you bring some play into your life? Find a way to play a game. Indoors or outdoors. Short or long. Alone or with someone else. It rediscovers the child within and is most liberating.

# 11

## *What can I do when my church lets me down?*

### *Problem*

The Church has a good track record in caring for people. Christian churches have for centuries cared for those who are unwell or marginalized. Many hospitals were initially founded through churches and monasteries. Healing is an important part of the Church's ministry to the world, and much of Jesus' recorded life is about his engaging with and bringing healing to the ill and distressed.

For many people today suffering from ill health the local church provides support in both practical and prayerful terms. Many churches have wonderful pastoral people who visit the sick and housebound, bringing contact and fellowship and often helping out in practical ways – doing shopping, providing transport to and visiting in hospital, offering meals, gardening and so on. Church congregations regularly pray for those unwell and many churches offer prayer for healing either after services or at special services for healing.

However, it has to be said that this support is often much more apparent for those suffering from physical illnesses and conditions rather than for those with emotional and mental health problems. Certainly among those who shared their stories with us this was often the case.

Christine and her husband had had depression for some years but didn't feel cared for by the church. When both she and her husband developed cancer, the church community was much more supportive of them. She said that church members found it hard to relate to and understand depression.

\* \* \*

Michael became very stressed and 'burnt out' in his early thirties. This wasn't surprising as he was stretched at home, work and church without adequate rest. At home he had a busy young family of four children, at work he was working long hours being inducted into the family business. He was a committed church member running a popular youth club and also taking services in the local area. As the stress built up he found himself unable to attend church at all. He would set out to go to church, only to be overwhelmed by nausea and needing to return home. The minister and many of the congregation were unsympathetic, someone telling him to 'pull himself together'. Although he didn't lose his faith in God he became disillusioned by the church.

Sadly the great strain he was under was unrecognized by the church and he felt very isolated from it by his difficulties and blamed for not being able to get better and get back to church. This lack of real understanding is not uncommon and was a recurring theme in people's stories.

\* \* \*

Sarah was in her forties when she was incapacitated by stress. She was a busy farmer's wife and very involved in her local church, being on many rotas and also vice chairman of the PCC and responsible during an interregnum. She was younger than many church members and full of energy.

About this time a dear friend of hers died and other close friends divorced. While she was grieving she had to have a hysterectomy, when in fact she might have liked to have more children. Her two children then went off to boarding school. A combination of these many losses, together with a difficult relationship with her mother-in-law and sister, resulted in Sarah developing a range of physical symptoms – panic attacks, palpitations, irregular heartbeat, total mental and physical exhaustion, tension – for which she had extensive medical investigations, though no underlying illness was found.

She tried to reduce her overload by asking to come off some church rotas and was met with a 'total lack of kindness or understanding'. No one from church asked what had happened or how she was. 'It would appear that I was only a consideration when I was working. Hence I became totally disillusioned and disenchanted with the whole set up and remain to this day pretty uninvolved in church.'

Fortunately her disillusionment did not affect her relationship with God. Sarah's personal faith grew over this time. 'For me such a wilderness time heightened my awareness and need of God and he was my absolute mainstay.'

Sarah used self-help books to try and understand what was happening to her. Her advice to other Christians suffering from stress is to find the right person to talk things through with, someone who will walk alongside you.

But it is salutary and sad to see how the lack of understanding of her difficulties and concern for her by the local church has led to her becoming a very marginal member of the congregation, when she might have been supported and then been able in turn to support others.

For Michael it turned out differently. He was given an enormous amount of support from his wife, saw his GP and took medication. However, he really began to get better when a new minister came to the church, visited him and prayed with him. Michael had a new and deeper experience of God's love, grace and strength for him, which brought healing. He was able to return to church and in time pick up roles there. He feels that today there is a better understanding in churches about the effects of stress but still inadequate support for those at risk of stress-related illnesses. The visit of the new minister, his acceptance, concern and support were instrumental in helping Michael get back to church and remain deeply involved.

Why is it that churches can be bad at giving adequate support in cases of stress and poor emotional and mental health? We think there are several reasons.

First, as Christine says, people find it very difficult to relate to mental problems as compared to physical difficulties and don't know how to help. Of course, this is not limited to churches and much work has been undertaken nationally to combat the stigma of mental illness. In recent years several world-class sportspeople and athletes have been able to reveal their battles with stress-related difficulties that have profoundly affected their ability to compete, and may have ended their sporting careers.

Second, stress-related problems can resolve quickly but can also last a long time. Therefore when people are offering support of some kind they are not always prepared for the long haul and can become frustrated with someone who doesn't seem to be improving, and blame them for not getting better when in fact it is part of the illness process.

Third, it is well recognized that most of the work of running a church is being done by a small minority and is not shared evenly across the church membership. Stress-related problems often occur in people at the busy heart of the church who have taken on many jobs, but those around them are also busy and working very hard. So when someone has to step down because of stress, although others feel sympathy there is also a realization that they may have to work harder to cover his or her absence. Often those at the heart of the church do not have either the time or the energy to offer the support needed. Other church members may think that they are not as close to the stressed person, or make the assumption that other people are doing the caring. Hence it is easy to see how we might begin to feel neglected and let down by the church if we become overstressed and have to stop fulfilling all our roles.

## *Opportunity*

Here is a chance to think back over our church involvement and see if we feel that we have been let down in any way by our church family or the Church at large. It would be helpful to put into words what we are feeling, rather than have the emotion sloshing around inside us. Perhaps taking time to write down in our journal what we feel we would like to have been done to support us more helpfully will be a starting point. What would we have appreciated someone doing for us? Was it visiting us, offering lifts, meals, childcare or someone simply listening to our story and seeking to understand? At what point did we begin to feel upset or resentful and angry?

Let's also aim to jot down any support we did have, even if it wasn't all we had hoped for or expected.

## Forgiveness

If we discover that we are harbouring anger or resentment against individuals or groups within the church, we might like to think about how we can start to forgive them. Forgiveness is a central theme in the New Testament but something that can be very difficult and costly to do when it involves us and our local church. Whole books are written about forgiveness and here we simply wish to flag it up as a challenge, because to be able to forgive liberates both parties and releases a lot of energy being used to hold on to hurt and resentment.

## Education

As those who have undergone such stresses as these, we have an opportunity to educate our church about stress and its consequences. It might be that if we have found some book or practice very helpful in alleviating our stress, we could share it with others in the church. Similarly we could look around us to see if anyone else is under a great deal of stress and pressure and try to encourage them in a small way. We may be in a position to organize and rally practical support for them. Often church members are unaware of the need or, if aware, do not know what overtures would be helpful. We are ideally placed to give advice about this. Obviously this would be something we get involved in as we recover from our own period of overstress, but perhaps we can begin to see how our own experiences may be preparing us to help others in future, rather than letting them feel forgotten and useless in the church.

## *Inspiration*

If this chapter is applicable to you and you feel you were let down by your church when you needed help because you were very stressed, be heartened. Others have gone before you.

Helen Jones suffered with cancer and when she couldn't find a support group to belong to, she started one.[1] Rachel Costa suffered from depression during her teens and set up a charity, Think Twice, which now runs courses for churches on mental health awareness. She says 'We need to make it more normal for churches to reach out in the same way that we would when someone's physically unwell.'[2]

You may be pleased and surprised to learn that there are several organizations that have come into being relatively recently to seek to improve and resource churches' understanding of emotional problems. One in particular will be mentioned here: Mind and Soul. This is a non-denominational organization exploring Christianity and mental health. On their website they write about themselves thus:

> In many churches and health care settings Christianity and mental health are kept deliberately separate. Mental health is rarely discussed in our churches and Christian spirituality is seen as having little to offer the world of psychology. At Mind and Soul we are seeking to bridge this gap and provide a place of integration for orthodox Christianity and high quality psychology and psychiatry . . .
>
> We want to support:
>
> - People who have a mental health problem but also have a strong Christian faith that they often find to be ignored.
> - Church leaders who need support with their emotional health and seek deeper understanding of mental health issues.
> - People who work in secular counselling or mental health services and want to see their Christian faith applied there.
> - Churches who want support in integrating a mental health agenda within their fellowship/teaching or pastoral care.
> - People who care about 'the poor' and want to reduce the stigma and suffering of people with mental health issues.[3]

If you want to help begin educating your church about emotional and mental health issues and how they impact on people and faith, look at this and other websites listed in the Resources section.

## Meditation

'Get rid of all bitterness, rage and anger . . . Be kind and compassionate to one another, forgiving each other, just as in Christ God forgave you' (Ephesians 4.31–32).

'Praise be to the God and Father of our Lord Jesus Christ, the father of compassion and the God of all comfort, who comforts us in all our troubles, so that we can comfort those in any trouble with the comfort we ourselves receive from God' (2 Corinthians 1.3–4).

These two verses fit with our opportunities section. Paul was writing to two different churches, one in Ephesus and the other in Corinth. Both had their difficulties and issues. We tend to suppose it would have been easier to forgive other church members in the early church but I suspect it was not. Paul reminds those at Ephesus to get rid of resentment and to be compassionate to each other, remembering that God has forgiven our sins because of Jesus and that we should do the same to others.

Paul reminds the Christians in Corinth that they can comfort – or strengthen, as the Greek word means – others in similar situations with the same strengthening God has given them.

Consider again whether there are those whom you need to forgive. Can you take a step towards doing that? Consider too if there is someone you could comfort or strengthen by sharing what you have learnt.

## Stressbuster: get into your body

All too often we can live in our heads, thinking or worrying a lot and going round in circles. The aim of this Stressbuster is to become more aware of our bodies and do something pleasurable that connects us to our skin and muscles.

> Although it was some years since she had been, Jacquie decided to go swimming every week and discovered there was a ladies-only night at her local pool. This gave her confidence not to worry what she looked like. She found herself really enjoying the swimming and came home more relaxed than she had felt for a long time. She then noticed that she could get a massage in the leisure centre and booked herself in for one each month. It made a real difference to her.

Try massage, swimming, sunbathing, just wearing less and going barefoot when you can. Enjoy sex as fully as you can. Have luxurious baths. Be as sensual as you can. Mostly we are badly out of touch with our bodies, and yet we can get a real sense of relaxation and unwinding when we give ourselves permission to focus on them.

*Part 5*

WORK

Part 5

WORK

# 12

## *How can I carry on when I feel swamped and disillusioned at work?*

### Problem

The workplace can seriously contribute to stress levels for everyone but there are particular issues for Christians, who want to work hard at serving the Lord in their jobs. This is not to say that many who share other beliefs are not also at risk of overstress because of their work ethics.

*First, whatever the line of work, Christians in general are committed to their work, are hard-working, idealistic and conscientious.* This is because of their underlying belief that they are really working for God and to please him, not simply their employer. As a result of their hard work and reliability they may be given more responsibility and be prepared to push themselves to ensure work gets done. They may end up feeling swamped, overloaded and not know where to turn.

Because of the economic downturn/austerity of the first four years of this decade, from 2010 onwards, resources to do a job have often been stretched very thin although despite this, staff are expected to maintain the same high-quality service. Workers are expected to manage with reduced administrative and managerial support, and often have training opportunities reduced. This can make what was a once manageable job feel very burdensome, and can result in feelings of disillusionment and exhaustion.

On top of this the culture of accountability has increased the amount of paperwork/electronic notes that have to be completed on a daily basis, which also distorts the shape of the job. Work practice, targets and ethos change over time and it may happen that as time goes by we feel unable to do the job we once did. We may find we have changes imposed on us from above and that we have very little say in the direction our work is taking. Our ideals may be very different from those of the management, and there may be little we can do to change that. If we are in middle management we may be required to present ideas we fundamentally disagree with to the workforce, which puts us in a very uncomfortable position. This happened to Joe when a new manager was appointed who wanted to make several changes. Joe didn't feel listened to when he put his views forward, but was expected to talk enthusiastically to the team below him about changes that were taking place. He felt compromised and caught in the middle, which added to his stress. And we may not be able to resign for many reasons. For the idealistic Christian this change in ethos can bring disillusion in its wake.

A further factor is the change in work expectations on availability. In many jobs there is an expectation that we will read and respond to work emails at all times of day (or night!). The advent of smartphones brings with it the difficulty of switching off from work and having adequate downtime when we are away from the workplace. Until fairly recently, when we left work we could forget about it overnight or over the weekend – unless on call – and have some time to rewind, but we may now feel obliged to check emails or be contactable at all times, which affects our recovery time.

*Second, Christians are often drawn to work in the caring professions*: teaching, healthcare, social work, policing, the mission field or full-time ministry. They care about and want to work with people and are highly dedicated, prepared to undergo, if necessary, years of training in their particular field. They want to 'change the world' and believe that with God's help they will. This idealism is highly commendable. As well as the stress arising from poor resourcing and high expectation issues mentioned above, working with people is never easy or straightforward. Measuring what has been achieved is much more difficult than in a commercial business, and people are notoriously stubborn at accepting and responding to help. There is always a vast sea of need and it can be very difficult to take time away from work to recuperate. Often our time away from work may also involve caring for people at home. It is not surprising that we begin to feel swamped and overstressed.

The combination of high ideals, responsibility at work with limited resources, a changing ethos and insufficient recovery time all take their toll and make us feel disillusioned and at the end of our tether.

These feelings are warning signs we do well to take seriously. They are symptoms of the stress we are under at work, not signs that we are backsliding Christians who simply need a kick up the backside to work harder, which is often how people do respond when they feel things slipping and swamping them at work. Understanding why we feel as we do, what are the particular pressures and stresses upon us, may help us see a way forward or what we might need to change in order to retain our ability to work effectively and productively with job satisfaction.

# Opportunity

When we recognize how stressed we are feeling because of our work situation, this may be the prompt that makes us determined to do something about it.

Of course, it is very unlikely that we will be in a position to quit or to change our job, for a whole host of reasons, and there is no guarantee that we will fare any better in a new workplace. What we can do is take this time as an opportunity to learn how to make life liveable and bearable where we are. It is a time to take steps to change our inner responses and learn how to live with all the difficulties while still maintaining an inner sense of calm and well-being. One way to approach this is to meditate or centre ourselves.

## Meditation and centring prayer

It is well recognized that stress levels can be reduced by meditation, and that the regular practice of meditation increases a person's inner sense of well-being. Meditation conjures up all sorts of images of eastern mysticism and it may not be something you think is helpful to Christians. It is worth saying that all the world's major religions have developed systems of meditation that bring people closer to their spiritual centre, and that there is a strong and well-established Christian tradition of meditation that has been practised down the centuries. Sometimes it is known as contemplative or centring prayer.[1]

The aim is to be stilled before God – 'Be still, and know that I am God' (Psalm 46.10) – and to allow our inner fragmented minds and thoughts to become centred and still, so that our spirit receives from the Spirit of Jesus. It is very simple to practise.

We can begin by sitting comfortably with our eyes closed and focusing on our breathing, noticing the rhythm of our breathing in and out. We may wish to say to ourselves 'Jesus' as we inhale; as we exhale, we let go of our worries and concerns. We should aim to do this for at least five minutes. Without doubt our thoughts will scatter all over the place, but each time we notice we are drifting away we should refocus on our breathing, gently bringing our attention back. This will become easier with practice. Some people like to use a candle or a stone as a focal point but it doesn't matter whether you choose a word, an object or your breathing – simply use it to refocus on inner stillness.

As time goes by we may wish to spend longer in silence and stillness, and a suggested practice is gradually to build up to two 20-minute periods each day. However, it is important to learn to walk before we run, so if we manage two 5-minute periods, we are doing well.

Do not become frustrated with yourself if your thoughts wander. Training your mind to be stilled is like training any wild creature – it needs time, patience and kindness. As we become still in body we realize how frenetic our conscious thoughts are. A helpful image is to imagine our thoughts as boats moving along a canal – we should simply let them move through the landscape, rather than try to suppress them. If we become aware that we are following a particular train of thought we need to refocus and let the thought go. Because of drifting thoughts and attention, our periods of contemplation may feel fruitless and pointless, but over time we begin to notice that we are reaping the rewards in other areas of our lives. We are less stressed and hassled at work, even when outer circumstances remain unchanged.

## Inspiration

Steve was a Christian and a committed teacher. In his mid-thirties he applied for a job as a deputy head at a secondary school and was delighted when he was offered the job. However, it proved more difficult than he had anticipated and the ethos in the school was different from at his previous one. He had been appointed to the post over the acting deputy head, who was sore about this and therefore unhelpful. The head teacher was under a lot of stress himself and seemed unaware of Steve's difficulties. Steve was given the task of making eight staff redundant, which he found very difficult and over-whelming. He had not been in his new post for very long when he began to experience symptoms of stress. He began to feel an under-lying anxiety about everything, and lost his appetite. His sleep was disturbed and he would wake in the night with a racing heart, worry-ing about school issues. He found himself unable to unwind and relax at weekends or even during the school holidays, and his family noticed he was more irritable and touchy with them, and tired all the time.

Eventually Steve recognized he was suffering from stress and did his own research into stress management. He started to try and change a few small things to make life more bearable. He didn't wish to change his job. Instead he booked himself activities to look forward to, like holidays. When he couldn't sleep he used the time to read light books or enjoy music, and tried not to worry so much about his lack of sleep. As time went by he got more on top of his job and found it less stressful. His symptoms improved and his attitude to his work changed.

## *Meditation*

We are writing this in the autumn of 2014, as Britain is being battered by storms and winds whipping up enormous, powerful and destruc-tive waves, and many are experiencing the misery of flooded homes. Vivid images have been in the media of huge waves, flooded streets and houses.

The sense of feeling overwhelmed and swamped is frequently linked to water in the Bible. In Psalm 69.1–3, David writes:

Save me, O God, for the waters have come up to my neck. I sink in the miry depths, where there is no foothold. I have come into the deep waters; the floods engulf me. I am worn out calling for help; my throat is parched. My eyes fail, looking for my God.

That this does not simply refer to actual flood waters is clear from verse 14, 'deliver me from those who hate me, from the deep waters'. The psalm is clearly about David feeling beset by hostile people and overwhelmed by their determination to destroy him, but he describes well the sense of feeling swamped and overwhelmed. Does this reson-ate with you? We too use the phrase 'I can't keep my head above water' in a similar way.

Isaiah 43.2 gives a promise: 'When you pass through the waters, I will be with you.' The disciples didn't feel God's presence when on a boat on the Sea of Galilee. A furious storm comes on the lake and the waves sweep over the boat so that it is nearly swamped (Mark 4.37). Is God with them? Yes, but asleep in the stern! The disciples fear that they are going to drown but instead witness Jesus as Lord of the wind and waves. They cry out to him, as does the psalmist. God is present with us in the middle of all our pressure and stress. We often forget that or wonder why he doesn't prevent the difficulties happening or smooth our way for us in the workplace.

A favourite photograph of ours is of a lighthouse keeper standing in the doorway of his lighthouse while an enormous wave, almost the height of the lighthouse, sweeps over the lighthouse from behind. He is safe and secure from it where he is standing. It reminds us of Proverbs 18.2: 'The name of the Lord is a fortified tower.'

We need to call on God in our workplace and pray for his presence and help there. We need to remember that he is with us and not be afraid to disturb him. Perhaps using times of meditation will make us more deeply aware of this truth.

## Stressbuster: nice surroundings

When I have been particularly stressed it has felt good to visit a spiritual director or accompanier. One of the most helpful things is that they have often put some thought into the room we meet in. It is usually simply furnished, with a few objects to focus on like a candle or some flowers. For me it is soothing not to be in my own clutter – it gives me head-space and I (Elizabeth) feel more relaxed.

This Stressbuster is to make your surroundings pleasant to be in – your home or your room, your garden or yard, your work space (if you are allowed to). Decorate them caringly. Make them a pleasure to be in. Make it so that they minister to you rather than make you feel more stressed. If it feels too outfacing or impractical to do things on a large scale, possibly make a corner where you find spiritual sanctuary, which is pleasantly laid out with shells, driftwood, candles, an icon or something with meaning for you, like the photo of the lighthouse keeper mentioned above.

# 13

## *How do I live out my Christian life at work?*

---

### *Problem*

As well as feeling swamped at work and becoming disillusioned and worn down, there can be other difficulties in the workplace for the Christian. A more secular and pluralistic society in Britain has brought with it a waning of influence of Christian teaching. In recent years and months we have seen a shift in society's perceptions of and an intolerance towards Christian practices that were once acceptable and not questioned.

### Symbols

Christian symbols, once commonplace in schools and hospitals, are conspicuously absent. Many Christians like to wear decorative crosses on chains round their necks. Often received at baptism or confirmation, they have particular meaning, as well as symbolizing that one is a Christian. Thousands of Christians have worn crosses for hundreds of years. In 2006 Nadia Eweida, a check-in clerk for British Airways at Heathrow airport, was disciplined and sent home for wearing a cross on a chain at work. She fought a legal battle over this and in 2013 the European Court of Human Rights upheld her right to wear a cross. However, in the same ruling a nurse lost her appeal after she had been asked to remove a cross and chain at work. Because the NHS Trust cited health and safety reasons, the ruling supported the Trust.

### Prayers

Christian prayers to start the day in schools, hospitals and local council meetings were the norm for many years. This is no longer the case. In the past it would not have been unusual, and indeed was often welcomed, for nurses and doctors to offer to pray with or for their patients. Yet in 2009 Caroline Petrie, a nurse, was suspended from work for offering to pray for an elderly patient. She was accused of failing to 'demonstrate a professional commitment to equality and diversity', but was later reinstated in her post. This episode provoked a national debate about the role of spiritual care in the healthcare services generally. In 2011 the General Medical Council (GMC) issued a statement to say that 'tactful offers to pray for patients could be appropriate'. Spirituality is viewed as important, but great sensitivity is required to interpret how we work with clients and patients in practice.

## Witness

Talking about our faith to colleagues can be difficult too, and often after mentioning that we go to church we may be the butt of jokes or watched more closely than our other colleagues. In 2013 someone was disciplined at work for expressing his Christian views about same-sex marriage on Twitter. A colleague had complained. Posts on social media websites and Twitter are often the cause of people not getting interviews or being disciplined, but we must stress that this is not particular to Christian content. Talking about our faith to people in our care can be a minefield. In 2012 Richard Scott, a Christian GP from Margate, was given a formal warning by the GMC for talking about Christianity with a patient, whose mother later complained about this. He has yet to go to appeal.

## Ethics

Christian ethics can also lead to difficulties and pressures at work. We may have different standards of practice from some of our colleagues. In some workplaces fiddling expenses is standard practice. We may be marked out as someone who acts differently. Our own understanding of Christian teaching may be in conflict with society's values. In 2013 a Christian couple who ran a bed and breakfast lost their legal battle in the Supreme Court not to be required to rent rooms to same-sex couples. It was ruled that they were running a business, even if from their own home, and that they therefore could not discriminate against same-sex couples.

Whatever we personally feel about the rights and wrongs of each particular scenario, there is no doubt that the freedom to express one's Christian faith at work has been seriously eroded and can feel like walking on eggshells. What is or is not acceptable? How do we live out our Christian faith in the workplace? How do we witness to the good news of the gospel to our colleagues and not prejudice our livelihoods? It can feel like a tightrope walk, trying to get it right, being caring and loving without being politically incorrect. This piles on the pressure. The workplace begins to feel like an alien place, one where we must express ourselves carefully. We are not used to living in this kind of environment in the West, though in many parts of the globe Christians are in a minority and seriously persecuted for their faith.

## *Opportunity*

When you are struggling at work and feeling under pressure, it is a good time to ask yourself some questions about your job.

- Why are you doing the job you're doing?
- Was it something you chose to do?
- Was it a job you had little choice about?
- Who influenced you in taking that particular job?
- Was it just convenient at the time?
- Did you always intend to move on but haven't got round to it?
- Did you feel a real calling to do the job, feel that God had opened a door for you?
- Did you have an inner conviction that you were in the right place, doing what God wanted you to do?
     If so, has anything changed?
     Is it still the right place?
     Have you felt a nudge to move on and tried to ignore it or feel it is too risky?
- Do you still feel in the right place but wish for a change?

It is helpful to ask ourselves these questions and try to answer them honestly. As ever, it is best to take the time to write your answers in your journal as it gives a greater level of engagement with the issues.

And again, it would be good to discuss your thoughts about your workplace stress levels with your spiritual accompanier.

## Salt and light

We may feel it is right to stay put despite the difficulties we face. If so we can take comfort from being salt and light (Matthew 5.13–16). There is a great deal to be said for a Christian presence in a dire situation. We can pray for our workplaces, not only for ourselves but for justice and equality for all the workforce. We can seek to live out our Christian values as best we can. We can be trustworthy and reliable employees, seeking to be constructive and not destructive.

If we do decide to remain where we are we may need to think very hard about what we can do to make our situation bearable. Once when I was very stressed at work, felt swamped and paralysed and didn't know how to keep going, I remembered the story of the four friends who carried the lame man to Jesus, even damaging the roof to lay him at Jesus' feet. I had the idea of asking four friends to agree to pray for me and about the situation. It was so immensely releasing and helpful, and I felt the burden lift. I did feel something inside of me shift and enable me to carry on and get through. Are there four friends you could approach who would regularly pray for you?

We may find that we can join a support group in our particular field. Several professional groups have a Christian fellowship, and talking to others who understand our work situation and will pray or give advice can be very sustaining. Or it may be something more simple, like taking a regular lunch or coffee break. Whatever – in order not to grind to a complete halt we should try to take at least one small step. What are *you* going to try?

## A new adventure

However, it may be that as we ask ourselves why we are in a particular job, we realize that it is time to move on and seek something new, possibly something altogether different. Now is the time to daydream, to let our thoughts roam to what we really want to do with our lives. We need to give ourselves permission to think outside the box. Then, when we have these ideas, comes the time for a reality check. Can we make these dreams come true? We will want to talk over our ideas with close family and friends. We need to think about the financial implications. Maybe, just maybe, God is asking us to step out in faith on a new adventure, to try a new thing. Or maybe now is not the right time to take these plans forward and they will need to be shelved for a while. But at least you have thought about them and there may come a time when you are able to bring them to fruition.

## Inspiration

In his book *Christians in the Firing Line*, Richard Scott[1] – the Christian GP we mentioned above – writes about 13 different cases of people who have been dismissed from work or penalized for practising their faith at work. He mentions the growth and beginnings of Christian Concern.[2] This organization was founded in 2008 by Andrea Minichiello Williams, a barrister, and grew out of the Lawyers' Christian Fellowship. Christian Concern works to defend Christians in the public sphere and protect the freedom of Christians to live their lives in accordance with their Christian beliefs. It has a sister organization called the Christian Legal Centre, and part of their remit is to provide legal representation in the courts for Christians who in the course of their professional lives have run into trouble with the authorities through practising their Christian faith at work. The Christian Legal Centre took on the cases of the people mentioned in the problem sector of this chapter, and have a lot of expertise in the legal difficulties within each case. Apparently hundreds of people now contact them every year for help. The Resources section at the end of the book gives information on how to contact them – it may be helpful to look at the website and read about the work they do.

But not all witnessing has to be so problematic, and here are two stories of Christians being salt and light in their workplace.

Eleanor was a member of one of our churches. She was a shy person, quiet, not one to push herself forward. She had had an administrative job for some years in a local university. Her office was open-plan, shared with some 20 others. She enjoyed the work and the atmosphere in the office. Her work colleagues were friendly and easy-going. A new female colleague was appointed to the office who was not unpleasant in any other way than that her language was bad. She swore every other word. This had not been the case with anyone in the office before. Eleanor found this offensive but didn't like to say anything. She wasn't sure her colleagues felt the same – no one else had said anything about it. Also she was not one for confrontation. She included the problem in her prayers and decided to say something to her new colleague about how she found her swearing offensive and would rather she did not do it. She did this in the hearing of all, very much fearing the reactions all round. She found she had a pleasant surprise. The woman concerned, the new colleague, took it very well. She had had no idea that her way of speaking, entirely natural to her, could be offensive. She was sorry if this was so, and was happy to cut out the swearing in future. Furthermore others in the office chimed in to say they hadn't liked the swearing either but hadn't wanted to cause upset by saying anything. They were glad Eleanor had spoken up. In fact the overall consensus in the office was to this effect. The whole thing was happily addressed early on. What could have been a running problem was nipped in the bud, with good relations maintained all around.

This is a small matter but testifies to the power of being prepared to stand up for what we believe in at work when something important is at stake. It might be surprising who else is won over by our doing that.

Another example of a different aspect to being a witness at work is provided by Tom, who was also shy and reticent by nature. He was a keen Christian and had always beaten himself up that he never had the courage to speak out for Jesus at work. He had worked in the same job for many years and never won one colleague for Christ in that time. His tradition was evangelical and his church had the expectation that members would witness boldly out in the world and win converts. Because he was so shy but felt he ought to be doing something at work, he got an evangelical bumper sticker for his car that said 'One Way', meaning that Jesus was the only way to life. It had a graphic on it that combined an upward-pointing arrow and a cross to get this over. Tom regularly gave lifts to work for different people who came from his district, and he hoped the sticker would catch their attention as a kind of compromise between speaking to them about Jesus directly and keeping quiet. Sadly nobody took him up in conversation about this sticker for a long time. Tom pretty much forgot it was there – until one day at the end of work, when his car got stuck in first gear and wouldn't reverse. His workmate, to whom he was giving a lift home that night, had to help him push his car out of its parking place as it would only go one way. 'Ah,' said his friend, 'Now I know what your sticker means!'

## *Meditation*

Life and work can be hard and at times unfair. The story of Joseph in Genesis 37 and 39—48 is a clear example of this. Joseph was an intelligent, tactless and lively young man, the pride and favourite of his father. He is betrayed and sold into slavery by his jealous half-brothers, and finds himself taken out of his country and working as a slave in Potiphar's household in Egypt. He is in a completely different culture and has lost his freedom and status. Despite this he works very hard and reliably, is noticed and promoted until he is in charge of all household matters. He had been dealt a very raw deal but he had made the best of it.

He also comes to the notice of Potiphar's wife, who repeatedly tries to seduce him. A victim of sexual harassment, he is honest and loyal to his master and avoids her when he can, but she ultimately accuses him of attempted rape. Her story is believed and Joseph is falsely imprisoned. Even in prison he again works hard for the prison guard, is helpful to Pharaoh's baker and butler in their time of need and asks to be remembered by them when they leave prison.

Sadly he is forgotten and let down, left to linger in prison for a couple of years more until the butler remembers his help in interpreting dreams. Once again Joseph's great qualities are spotted by Pharaoh, he is promoted and becomes his right-hand man, in time overseeing a food distribution programme and saving the lives of his brothers and his family – those who had earlier betrayed him into a life of slavery. Life treated him unjustly and unfairly both within the family and also in work situations.

Despite this he makes the best of things, somehow doesn't become embittered and is able to say 'You intended to harm me, but God intended it for good to accomplish what is now being done, the saving of many lives' (Genesis 50.20).

Joseph's story is a challenging one for us all. When we are falsely accused and the victim of injustice at work, how do we take it? Are we able to go on giving our best? If we have a new boss we don't really want, are we able to continue to work well for him of her in the right spirit? It doesn't mean that we collude with injustice, nor that we don't put our side of a story. But having done so, when the outcome maybe isn't what we hoped for, can we get on with life anyway, making the best of our circumstances and believing that God has a plan, maybe a very long-term plan, and that we can trust him? Joseph's story can give us hope in dark situations.

## *Stressbuster: treats*

Treat yourself from time to time, at least weekly. Find something nice you would really enjoy. It needn't be anything elaborate or expensive: a long bath, a coffee at your favourite coffee shop, a walk, sitting down to read a good book, watching an undemanding TV programme or film, watching a football or rugby match, playing darts in the local pub – anything that would be enjoyable for you. Make an oasis of pleasure in your week that is going to be there to look forward to, and will be some proper downtime and help you switch off from all the surrounding stressors. If you are stuck, think what you would suggest to another colleague undergoing stress and then use you own suggestion.

> John began to support his local rugby team and went along to their matches. He said that he found cheering for his team very cathartic and that it released a lot of stress. Brian was a full-time carer for his wife but found that a weekly round of golf helped him unwind and enabled him to cope with the rest of the week. What would work for you?

*Part 6*

# CULTURE AND SOCIETY

# 14

## How can we keep our distinctiveness as Christians in today's society?

———————•◦•———————

### Problem

Among the factors that add to the particular stress in life for Christian people is the increasing indifference and even hostility to the Christian faith in larger society.

Within the lifetime of most people reading this book, the overall view of our society to Christianity has changed a great deal. The numbers of those attending church services on a regular basis have fallen dramatically. In 1980, UK church attendance was 11 per cent; by 2010 it was 6 per cent. The numbers of those calling themselves Christians in the national censuses has also fallen considerably (from 71.6 per cent in 2001 to 59.3 per cent in 2011), though it still stands at almost two-thirds of those responding in 2011. There has been increasing pressure from secularists to end practices like Christian prayer at local council meetings and the use of promises to God in uniformed organizations like the Guides and Scouts. There are no longer routinely Christian chaplaincies and chapels in institutions like our hospitals, prisons and the armed forces. It's now more likely to be a multifaith centre with a multifaith team of chaplains, not necessarily headed by a Christian.

Bishop Michael Nazir-Ali, in his book *Triple Jeopardy for the West*,[1] identifies three main areas of threat to our Christian culture. First, he talks about multiculturalism and the ways it's being used to dismantle our Christian ethic in society, so carefully built up over a millennium and a half. He talks about 'thin' values like tolerance and social parity as opposed to 'thick' values like the Christian ethic and the deeper understandings of faith and morality that are needed to hold a society together. Second, he talks about radical Islam and the foothold it has in the UK. No one is in a better position than him to understand it as a lifelong student of Islam and also of Pakistani origin. Recent cases in Birmingham and Bradford schools, where special measures have had to be taken to counteract Islamicizing influences coming from governors, illustrate the heightening pressures in this area – as does the worrying support for the Islamic State movement in Syria and Iraq shown by significant numbers of young Muslim Britons. Third, he talks about the militant atheism that is now fashionable. Richard Dawkins' book *The God Delusion*[2] has sold over a million copies. Dawkins himself enjoys a high profile, regularly appearing on the media. He was applauded to his place by the audience at a recent debate in the Cambridge union, though he lost the debate to the then Archbishop of Canterbury, Rowan Williams, in a motion about the existence of God, by two to one. There is even now the fashion of holding atheist services on Sunday mornings, which are gatherings akin to a religious service but without the belief.

A further aspect of this is that those holding distinctive beliefs are only tolerated so long as they accept that their beliefs are entirely subjective. It's all right to believe provided you don't inflict it on others. 'Proselytizing' has become a buzz word, as has 'sectarian'. For instance, local councils who once gladly supported specifically Christian local charities now fear to do so lest they lay themselves open to charges of supporting sectarian causes, no matter how long-standing or commendable the charities concerned. A Baptist minister preaching in the open air in his local town centre on the epistle to the Ephesians was taken into custody by the local police. No charges were made but it shows the fear of evangelism and the insistence that religion be kept a private matter. In a number of countries anti-conversion laws exist, usually to give a legal facade to the persecution of religious minorities. No such law exists in the UK as yet, but it is no longer unthinkable. The Incitement to Religious Hatred Act of 2011 has certainly given concern to some informed Christians that it is a step towards making the preaching of the primacy of Jesus Christ an illegal act.

All of this amounts to a cultural background that makes it very stressful to be a card-carrying Christian. We suspect that it accounts for more stress on Christians than we tend to realize.

Notwithstanding all this, we need to acknowledge that our modern culture is still very open to spirituality as such. Retreats, pilgrimages, interfaith dialogue, prayer and meditation events of all kinds have boomed at the same time as Christianity as the defining faith of the nation has waned. An example would be the huge increase in the numbers of people going on the Santiago de Compostela pilgrimage across northern Spain. Hundreds of thousands of people, many of them with no or very little formal Christian upbringing, walk lengths of the route all around the year. Our daughter and son-in-law went this year for a week while we looked after their three lively sons. It was a close thing who was the more tired afterwards, us or them! But they came back inspired by the variety of the people they'd met on the way. These ranged from an 86-year-old woman who had walked 600 miles, to a man who was walking because God had granted him the safe birth of a baby son, and many more. The Santiago de Compostela pilgrimage, an ancient mediaeval web of routes from all over Europe, is now the subject of a moving film, *The Way*, starring Michael Sheen as an agnostic man who walks as a way of mourning the death of his adult son. It's a good film, describing his change of outlook as he walks. You might like to watch it.

There is still, too, a reservoir of interest and sympathy with the Church of England at a grass-roots level. In the media, TV series like *Rev* and *Grantchester* are based on the lives of Anglican clergy sympathetically portrayed, as is the vicar in the two series of the thriller *Broadchurch*. And attendances at Cathedrals on a regular basis and in all churches at Christmas show serious increases.

## *Opportunity*

As ever, let's take these challenges in our anti-Christian culture as an opportunity. Once again, we suggest the use of journaling as you address living in a diverse culture. We think you would be rewarded by writing in your journal even just a few lines under each of the headings we now mention. Writing in this way will, we hope, clear your mind and help you come by a healthy perspective about modern life. It will also help you come to any decisions for action to do with this that you might want to take.

*First, we would do well to look at our culture and think of all there is that we appreciate about it.* It's arguable we in the West live in a better time and place than anybody in the whole of civilization, with our standards of healthcare, education, constitutional freedoms, life expectancy and opportunities for travel, among many other things. We ought to be grateful for these and take good stock of them before allowing ourselves to become overdespondent about the times in which we live. It would be good to write down our list of such good things and pray a prayer of appreciation for them.

*Second, whatever else, matters of faith are very much in the news.* Elizabeth and I go back to the 1970s, when the expectancy of the secular world was that religion would just quietly die a natural death by the end of the century. It was so anaemic and irrelevant in the secular world's eyes. People would move on and simply forget religion. Now scarcely a day goes by without the news and opinion pages of the daily papers carrying religious issues of one sort or another. This is an opportunity for us.

Third, a way of using all these challenges to the faith, whether through atheism or through other world faiths, is to *do some work about getting our own thinking clear about why we are Christians and not, for example, atheists, Muslims, Sikhs or Hindus.* There are a wealth of good, recent books about what's particular to Christian faith. And there are good replies from Christian authors to Professor Dawkins, as well as good books about a healthy relationship with the other world faiths. We give suggested titles in the Resources section.

*Fourth, it might be an opportunity to take action.* We still live in a democracy with freedom of speech. We're entitled to write to our MPs. We can campaign. There are a number of organizations campaigning right now for the retention of Christian standards in public life in a number of ways. Again, contact details for some of these organizations are in the Resources section. It may well be that looking at our anti-Christian culture stirs us into some right action.

*Fifth and finally, it's an opportunity to reach out to others around us.* Religion is very much on people's lips. People are thinking about faith issues for all kinds of reasons and it's a good opportunity to ask God for the chance to share with our acquaintances something of our own faith in Jesus.

## Inspiration

If we are tempted to fear what will become of our Christian faith if our country becomes more hostile to it, let's take heart from what is happening in China, where both government and culture are much more hostile.

China is on course to become the world's most Christian nation within 15 years.[3] The number of Christians in Communist China is growing so rapidly that by 2030 it could have more churchgoers than the USA. China's Protestant community, which had just one million members in 1949, has already overtaken those of countries more commonly associated with an evangelical boom. It is impossible to say how many Christians there are in China today, but no one denies the numbers are exploding. The government says 25 million, 18 million Protestants and six million Catholics. Independent estimates all agree this is a vast underestimate. A conservative figure is 60 million. There are already more Chinese at church on a Sunday than in the whole of Europe. In China it is estimated that there are now more self-avowed disciples of Jesus than members of the Communist party. Even the most conservative estimates suggest that China will soon have more Christians than any country.

## Meditation: Daniel 1—6

Daniel in the Old Testament provides us with a great example of someone who overcame being plummeted into a seriously hostile culture. He kept his faith and became a leading figure in the Babylonian society into which he had been taken captive. His story, in brief, is that together with his three associates he was among a major deportation of talented, intellectual youth from Jerusalem to Babylon. Once there he was required to be schooled in the practice of divination of the court of King Nebuchadnezzar. This would have been highly occult – if any of us had a young son, say of undergraduate age, schooling themselves in witchcraft we would be deeply concerned – but Daniel and his friends keep the purity of their faith through it. Daniel goes on to serve four different emperors as Chief Minister, refusing in various times and ways to compromise his practice of praying to God three times a day. His friends famously refused to bow down to the great golden image of the emperor and survive the holocaust into which they are thrown. In all this, Daniel retains his concern for the holy city, Jerusalem, the Temple and the plight of the people of God who Nebuchadnezzar deports wholesale after sacking Jerusalem.

We thoroughly recommend that you pick up a Bible and read the first six chapters of the book of Daniel, which give his story. The remainder of the book is of apocalyptic visions that are of immense insight and value in themselves, but the first six chapters give the feeling of the hostile culture in which Daniel had to live. We might note that key parts of his story involve regular prayer, a deep concern for Jerusalem and penitence about its loss, a readiness to fast and a willingness, when it really came to it, to defy even emperors for the sake of his God.

## Stressbuster: music

Our final Stressbuster is to listen to music. Music is a proven easer of stress. You might recall how in the Old Testament story King Saul used to have David play for him to ease his mental turmoil (1 Samuel 16.14–23). You don't have to be in as bad a state as Saul to find listening to music relaxing and at the same time energizing. It's never been easier to have music accessible to listen to just about wherever you are or whatever you are doing. Phone apps, iPods, iPads have all come in in recent years and open up ways to listen to music that weren't possible before. There's no particular type of music that works better than any other. It's just according to your taste. It needn't be Christian music, though many do find worship songs or classical sacred music inspiring. But it can just as easily be ordinary pop music, classics, jazz, rock, heavy metal – whatever. It need not even be music. We came by a friend who plays the video of her infant niece playing and laughing on her phone to get herself off to sleep when she is particularly tense.

# Conclusion

Thank you for reading this far, and hope you have found it instructive, inspiring and helpful. We certainly tried to make it so.

Stress is an important factor in twentieth-century living and affects many of us, whether Christian or not. We have seen how the very fact of being a Christian can increase our stress levels in certain ways. However, we hope that you have begun to appreciate that feeling stressed out can be a gateway to a more whole and more human way of life. It is not the end but a beginning – a chance to review and change harmful patterns of living, to explore new ways of being before God and in our life situation.

Perhaps you have been able to see more clearly that God is present and at work behind the scenes. You may have been reminded that his work is on a much larger scale than you had realized. Your place in it may not always make much sense to you, but in the eternal scheme of things God has a place for you and he knows what he is doing.

By way of an ending: we listened recently to the Archbishop of Canterbury, Justin Welby, on BBC Radio 4's *Desert Island Discs*, interviewed by Kirsty Young. We reckoned that if any Christian is going to be under stress it would be him, with his worldwide responsibilities and the intractable problems those bring with them. He frequently flies to troubled areas around the globe and was interviewed a few hours after arriving back from Southern Sudan. Not only that, but he has his own personal issues. He is the product of a broken home; his father was an alcoholic, and he explains in the programme how much this affected their family life. Also, he and his wife lost their first child, a baby girl, in a car crash. So he hasn't had it easy, nor has he got it easy now.

Naturally enough Kirsty asked him more than once how he copes with all the stress and how he replenishes himself emotionally and spiritually to do so. His replies are inspiring and – in our view! – chime in to a large degree with things we recommend in this book. He mentions:

- taking quiet moments through the day to tune into God;
- silent prayer;
- taking times of regular relaxation, such as days off and holidays;
- talking with his family and friends;
- playing games;
- having a pattern of regular, structured prayer and meditation;
- seeing all the positives in any given situation;
- exercise;
- routine (when possible).

You may want to listen to it – at the time of writing it is available as a podcast[1] – as a way to round off your reading of our book.

We end by leaving you with this Scripture from Acts 14.22. The words are those of Paul who, having founded the first gentile churches on his initial missionary journey through the Roman province of Asia (modern southern Turkey), returns to them on his way back to Palestine to appoint elders and leave them with an abiding message. He says, 'We must go through many hardships to enter the kingdom of God.'

Andrew was using the final chapter of a confirmation book with a teenage boy and his mother. It was on the subject of the kingdom of heaven. It showed a picture of a butterfly and a chrysalis. It made the point that the butterfly, having pupated from the caterpillar, goes through immense stress to break out of the carapace of the chrysalis, so much so that it nearly dies. Indeed, researchers were so moved when observing its sufferings that, on some occasions, they loosened the shells of the chrysalis slightly to ease the pain. But interestingly, those pupae whose shells they had loosened produced butterflies whose wings were improperly formed and could not sustain flight and so died. It was the ones whose shells had been left untouched and who went through the most sustained, painful stress which, when they did emerge, were best prepared for life as a butterfly, able to fly properly. So our stresses, huge and even life-threatening as they can be, can be seen as preparing us fully for God's kingdom in heaven.

# Resources

## Part 1 Stress

### General books on stress

Todd Duncan, *Life on the Wire: Avoid Burnout and Succeed in Work and Life*, Nashville, TN: Nelson, 2010.

Edward England, *The Addiction of a Busy Life*, Crowborough: Aviemore Books, 1998.

Bruce G. Epperly and Katherine Gould Epperly, *Feed the Fire: Avoiding Clergy Burnout*, Cleveland, OH: Pilgrim Press, 2008.

Ruth Fowke, *Personality and Stress: Finding Ways to Manage Your Stress*, Farnham: CWR, 2009.

Kate Middleton, *Stress: How to De-Stress Without Doing Less*, Lion Books, 2009.

Andrew and Elizabeth Procter, *The Essential Guide to Burnout: Overcoming Excess Stress*, Oxford: Lion Books, 2013.

### Personality indicator

Myers Briggs Type Indicator – see <www.myersbriggs.org>.

## Part 2 God

### Books on different ways to pray

Ruth Fowke, *Personality and Prayer: Finding and Extending the Prayer Style that Suits Your Personality*, Guildford: Eagle, 1997.

Margaret Hebblethwaite, *Finding God in all Things*, London: Fount, 1987.

Margaret Hebblethwaite, *Motherhood and God*, London: Geoffrey Chapman, 1984.

Brother Lawrence, *The Practice of the Presence of God*, Mineola, NY: Dover, 2005.

Wanda Nash, *Come, let us play! Playfulness and prayer*, London: Darton, Longman and Todd, 1999.

## Courses on Christian basics

Alpha offer a series of interactive sessions that freely explore the basics of Christian faith and other courses on Christian basics.

Alpha International
Holy Trinity Brompton
Brompton Road
Knightsbridge
London SW7 1JA
Tel: +44 845 644 7544
Website: www.alpha.org

## Books on Christian basics

William Barclay, *The Plain Man Looks at the Apostles' Creed*, London: Collins, 1967.
Nicky Gumbel, *Questions of Life*, Eastbourne: Kingsway, 2003.
Alister McGrath, *I Believe: Exploring the Apostles' Creed*, Leicester: Inter-Varsity Press, 1997.
John Stott, *Basic Christianity*, Nottingham: Inter-Varsity Press, 2008.

## Pilgrimage information

McCabe Pilgrimages is a tour company that offers Christian pilgrimage experiences to nine different destinations.

McCabe Pilgrimages
11 Hillgate Place
Balham Hill
London SW12 9ER
Tel: +44 208 675 6828
Website: www.mccabe-travel.co.uk/index.html

A good book for those considering pilgrimage is: Ian Bradley *Pilgrimage: A Spiritual and Cultural Journey*, Oxford: Lion, 2009.

## Short-term mission resource

OSCAR is the UK information service for world mission and provides a very helpful guide for those considering short-term mission service overseas.

OSCAR
Wotton House
Horton Road
Gloucester GL1 3PT
Tel: 0845 519 7732 or 01452 308189
Mobile: 07017467227
Email: info@oscar.org.uk
Website: www.oscar.org.uk/opportunity/shorttermmission.htm

## *Part 3 Family life*

Wendy Billington, *I'm Fine! Removing Masks and Growing into Wholeness*, Abingdon: BRF, 2013.

Care for the Family offers courses on parenting, both general courses (for new parents and for parents of older children) and specialist support for families with children with additional needs, step-families and single parents. They also run courses for engaged and married couples and bereavement courses for widows and bereaved parents and children.
Tel: 029 2081 0800
Website: www.careforthefamily.org.uk

Family Lives is a national charity providing help and support in all aspects of family life.
Helpline: 0808 800 2222
Website: www.familylives.org.uk

Family and Childcare Trust is an independent charity that exists to make the UK a better place for families and children. They work with charities, businesses and public services to offer practical help to families.

Family and Childcare Trust
2nd Floor
The Bridge
81 Southward Bridge Road
London SE1 0NQ

Tel: 0207 9407510
Website: www.familyandchildcaretrust.org

The Working Parent offers helpful information for parents who juggle work and family life.

The Working Parent
Littleworth Grange
South End
Goxhill
North Lincolnshire DN19 7NE
Tel: 01469 531413
Website: www.theworkingparent.com

Single Parents Action Network engage with and empower one-parent families.

Single Parents Action Network
The Silai Centre
176–178 Easton Road
Easton
Bristol BS5 0ES
Tel: 0117 955 0860 or 951 4231
Website: www.spanuk.org.uk

Happy Steps gathers together a range of services to help strengthen stepfamilies.
Tel: 07736 241542
Website: www.happysteps.co.uk

Gingerbread provide expert advice, practical support and campaign for single parent families.

Gingerbread
520 Highgate Studios
53–79 Highgate Road
London NW5 1TL
Website: www.gingerbread.org.uk

Divorce Care is an international initiative that has a strong Christian emphasis in its seminars and support groups, where leaders are people who understand the impact of divorce. Each session is based around one of 13 video presentations.

Tel: 919 562 2112 (international)

Website: www.divorcecare.com

Divorce Recovery Workshop includes a course of six weekly evening sessions or a weekend residential course. This self-help group is based around a series of videos that provide the opening for a discussion in small groups.

Divorce Recovery Workshop

11 Sewell Avenue

Wokingham

Berks RG41 1NT

Tel: 0700 078 1889

Website: www.drw.org.uk

The Couple Connection gives interactive information, advice, exercises and social networking for couples and parents.

The Couple Connection

1 Benjamin Street

London EC1M 5QG

Website: www.thecoupleconnection.net

The Five Love Languages help you find out about the love languages and discover how you can better communicate with your partner.

Email: info@5lovelanguages.com.

Website: www.5lovelanguages.com

See also:

Gary Chapman, *The 5 Love Languages: The Secret to Love that Lasts*, Chicago, IL: Northfield, 2010.

Marriage Care specialize in helping couples (married or not) build and sustain strong, fulfilling, healthy relationships, and in providing support in times of relationship difficulty.

Marriage Care
Bishops Park House
25–29 Fulham High Street
London SW6 3JH
Tel: 0207 371 1341
Website: www.marriagecare.org.uk

The Marriage Course is a seven-session course where couples can give their relationship an MOT through personal discussions. Courses are run throughout the UK. Relationship central website also contains links to a marriage preparation course, parenting children course and parenting teenagers course.
www.relationshipcentral.org/marriage-course

One plus One is the UK's leading relationship research organization. Their website provides online services to help couples and parents help themselves and resources to help frontline practitioners who support families with relationship issues. [1]
www.oneplusone.org.uk

Relate give advice, counselling, sex therapy, workshops, mediation, consultations, telephone and face-to-face support for all couples.
Tel: 0300 100 1234
Website: www.relate.org.uk

Time for Marriage offer marriage enrichment weekends at venues around the country.

Time for Marriage
21 Harvey Crescent
Warsash
Southampton
Hants SO31 9TA
Tel: 01798 345222
Email: admin@timeformarriage.org.uk
Website: www.timeformarriage.org.uk

On the phenomenon of sexting, see:
Stefan Kiesbye (ed.), *Sexting*, Detroit, MI: Greenhaven Press, 2011.

Worth Talking About can give you confidential advice if you think you may be pregnant.
Helpline: 0300 123 2930.

Sexual Advice Association (formerly the Sexual Dysfunction Association) is a charitable organization to help improve the sexual health and well-being of men and women and to raise awareness of the extent to which sexual conditions affect the general population.
Helpline: 0207 486 7262
Website: www.sda.uk.net

Sex Addiction Help is a free online self-help recovery resource for people struggling with sex or pornography.
www.sexaddictionhelp.co.uk

Two:23 is a network of Christians connected by LGBT (lesbian, gay, bisexual and transgender) issues who have discovered that God loves us just as we are. This realization frees us unashamedly to include and encourage all to discover the love of God for themselves, pursue the call of Christ and live in a way that cherishes others just as God cherishes us.
http://two23.net/about-two23

## *Part 4 Church life*

On starting a support group, see:
Pat Ashworth, 'Fellow travellers in the valley', *Church Times*, 17 October 2014 (about a cancer-support charity founded by Helen Jones, <www.firmroots.org.uk>).

Think Twice depression charity was born out of a personal struggle with mental illness. It exists to assist others in their own struggles and those who stand beside them. The charity's aim is to increase awareness and decrease stigma so that people are as able to be open about their mental health condition as they are about having the 'flu.
www.thinktwiceinfo.org

Mind and Soul is a non-denominational organization exploring Christianity and mental health who want to support (for more on Mind and Soul, see Chapter 11).

Premier Mind and Soul
22 Chapter St
London SW1P 4NP
Call Premier Lifeline for a listening ear, emotional and spiritual support and
confidential prayer: 0845 345 0707 or 0207 316 0808 – 9 a.m. to midnight
Website: www.mindandsoul.info

Mental Health Matters is a website for the Church of England to share
resources, best practice and advice on how churches can deal with mental
health issues.
www.mentalhealthmatters-cofe.org

For creative and constructive advice on conflict, see:
Joyce Huggett, *Conflict: Constructive or Destructive?*, Stowmarket: Kevin
   Mayhew, 2003.

## Part 5 Work

For case studies of people penalized at work for Christian practices,
see:
Richard Scott *Christians in the Firing Line*, London: Wilberforce, 2013.

Christian Concern and its sister organization the Christian Legal Centre
describe their purpose as 'to defend Christians in the public sphere and
to protect the freedom of Christians to live their lives in accordance with
their Christian beliefs'.

Christian Concern/Christian Legal Centre
70 Wimpole Street
London W1G 8AX
Tel: 0203 327 1120
Website: www.christianconcern.com/christian-legal-centre

## Part 6 Culture and society

### Books about Christianity, other faiths and atheism

Ida Glaser, *The Bible and Other Faiths: What Does the Lord Require of Us?*,
   Leicester: Inter-Varsity Press, 2005.

Alister McGrath and Joanna Collicutt McGrath, *The Dawkins Delusion? Atheist Fundamentalism and the Denial of the Divine*, London: SPCK, 2007.

Michael Nazir-Ali, *Triple Jeopardy for the West: Aggressive Secularism, Radical Islamism and Multiculturalism*, London: Bloomsbury, 2012.

Malcolm Torry, *Together and Different: Christians Engaging with People of Other Faiths*, Norwich: Canterbury Press, 2008.

Andrew Wilson, *Deluded by Dawkins? A Christian Response to the God Delusion*, Eastbourne: Kingsway, 2007.

Christian Concern, already mentioned in the section above relating to Part 5, provides free resources for retention of Christian standards in public life. They have free downloadable booklets in their online resources section – see <www.christianconcern.com/resources>.

## Organizations supporting persecuted Christians

Open Doors
PO Box 6
Witney
Oxon OX29 6WG
Tel: +44 01993 777300
Email: inspire@opendoorsuk.org
Website: www.opendoorsuk.org

Christian Solidarity Worldwide
PO Box 99
New Malden
Surrey KT3 3YF
Tel: +44 0845 456 5464
Email: admin@csw.org.uk
Website: www.csw.org.uk

Release International
PO Box 54
Orpington
BR5 4RT
Tel: 01689 823491
Website: www.releaseinternational.org

Barnabas Fund
9 Priory Row
Coventry CV1 5EX
Tel: 024 7623 1923
Website: http://barnabasfund.org

# *Notes*

## Introduction

1 *Work Stress*, a report (2012) published by the UK National Work-stress Network, p. 19; see <www.workstress.net>.
2 *Church Times*, 11 October 2013.

## 1 What is stress?

1 Joel Gascoigne, buffer.com, May 2014. Reproduced by kind permission.

## 2 How do I know if I'm overstressed?

1 Andrew and Elizabeth Procter, *The Essential Guide to Burnout: Overcoming Excess Stress*, Oxford: Lion, 2013, pp. 24–30.
2 Pablo Martinez, 'Caring for ourselves', *Triple Helix*, Winter 2013, pp. 6–7.

## 3 I know I'm overstressed but how do I stop?

1 Edward England, *The Addiction of a Busy Life*, Crowborough: Aviemore Books, 1998.
2 Andrew and Elizabeth Procter, *The Essential Guide to Burnout: Overcoming Excess Stress*, Oxford: Lion, 2013, p. 47. Extract from *The Essential Guide to Burnout* by Andrew and Dr Elizabeth Procter, published by Lion Hudson, 2013. Text copyright © 2013 Andrew and Dr Elizabeth Procter. This edition copyright © 2013 Lion Hudson. Used with permission.
3 Ruth Fowke, *Personality and Stress: Finding Ways to Manage Your Stress*, Farnham: CWR, 2009, p. 33.
4 England, *Addiction of a Busy Life*, pp. 156–7.
5 Robert Murray M'Cheyne, quoted in Pablo Martinez, 'Caring for ourselves', *Triple Helix*, Winter 2013, pp. 6–7.

## 4 How can I make time for God?

1 Ruth Fowke, *Personality and Stress: Finding Ways to Manage Your Stress*, Farnham: CWR, 2009, p. 33.
2 Margaret Hebblethwaite, *Motherhood and God*, London: Geoffrey Chapman, 1984, p. 101.

3 Brother Lawrence, *The Practice of the Presence of God*, Mineola, NY: Dover, 2005, p. 61.

4 Lawrence, *Practice of the Presence*, p. 23.

5 Lawrence, *Practice of the Presence*, p. 61; emphasis in original.

6 William Barclay, *The New Daily Study Bible: The Letter to Romans*, Louisville, KY: Westminster John Knox, 2002, pp. 184–5; emphasis in original.

## 5 How can I reconnect with God?

1 *Church Times*, 26 September 2014, p. 48.

2 *Church Times*, 19 September 2014, p. 7.

## 6 How can I manage my family life as a Christian?

1 Figure released by the Office for National Statistics in February 2014. See <www.ons.gov.uk/ons/taxonomy/index.html?nscl=Families>.

2 See <www.nationalcounsellingsociety.org/about/news/number-of-step-families-in-britain-increasing>.

3 Arielle Kuperberg, 'Does premarital cohabitation raise your risk of divorce?', Council on Contemporary Families, <https://contemporaryfamilies.org/cohabitation-divorce-brief-report>, March 2014.

4 *The Times*, 15 April 2014.

## 7 What am I to make of the sexual revolution?

1 See <www.kinseyinstitute.org/resources/FAQ.html#Age>.

2 *The Independent*, 18 October 2007.

3 Anne Mitchell, lead author of National Survey of Australian Secondary Students and Sexual Health, 2013, interviewed in *The Times*, 8 September 2014, p. 30. See also <www.latrobe.edu.au/news/articles/2014/release/teen-sexual-health-survey-launched>.

4 'Cohabitation and marriage in Britain since the 1970s', paper published in 2011 by the ESRC Centre for Population Change, University of Southampton.

5 According to Gavin Thompson et al., *Olympic Britain: Social and Economic Change Since the 1908 and 1948 London Games*, London: House of Commons Library, 2012, p. 18; available at <www.parliament.uk/documents/commons/lib/research/olympic-britain/olympicbritain.pdf>.

6 Office for National Statistics – see <www.ons.gov.uk/ons/taxonomy/index.html?nscl=Families>, then '13 Facts about divorce'.

7 *Daily Mail*, 17 December 2014.

8 See <www.foryourmarriage.com>.
9 *The Times*, 19 May 2014.

## 10 How do I cope with church politics?

1 The Churches' Ministerial Counselling Service – see <www.cmincs.net>.
2 Daniel Meyer, *Witness Essentials: Evangelism that Makes Disciples*, Downers Grove, IL: InterVarsity Press, 2012, pp. 32–3.

## 11 What can I do when my church lets me down?

1 Helen Jones, as reported in *Church Times*, 17 October 2014.
2 Rachel Costa, as reported in *Church Times*, 2 May 2014.
3 Mind and Soul – see <www.mindandsoul.info>.

## 12 How can I carry on when I feel swamped and disillusioned at work?

1 Thomas Keating, *Open Mind, Open Heart: The Contemplative Dimension of the Gospel*, Warwick, NY: Amity House, 1986, p. 18.

## 13 How do I live out my Christian life at work?

1 Richard Scott, *Christians in the Firing Line*, London: Wilberforce, 2013.
2 See <www.christianconcern.com>.

## 14 How can we keep our distinctiveness as Christians in today's society?

1 Michael Nazir-Ali, *Triple Jeopardy for the West: Aggressive Secularism, Radical Islamism and Multiculturalism*, London: Bloomsbury, 2012.
2 Richard Dawkins, *The God Delusion*, London: Bantam Press, 2006.
3 *The Telegraph*, 19 April 2014.

## Conclusion

1 See <www.bbc.co.uk/podcasts>.

## Did you know that SPCK is a registered charity?

As well as publishing great books by leading Christian authors, we also . . .

**. . . make assemblies meaningful and fun for over a million children** by running www.assemblies.org.uk, a popular website that provides free assembly scripts for teachers. For many children, school assembly is the only contact they have with Christian faith and culture, and the only time in their week for spiritual reflection.

**. . . help prisoners to become confident readers** with our easy-to-read stories. Poor literacy is a huge barrier to rehabilitation. Prisoners identify with the believable heroes of our gritty fiction. At the same time, questions at the end of each chapter help them to examine their choices from a moral perspective and to build their reading confidence.

**. . . support student ministers overseas in their training**. We give them free, specially written theology books, the International Study Guides. These books really do make a difference, not just to students but to ministers and, through them, to a whole community.

Please support these great schemes: visit www.spck.org.uk/support-us to find out more.